EDUCATION AND WORKING LIFE

ORGANISATION FOR ECONOMIC
CO-OPERATION AND DEVELOPMENT

The Organisation for Economic Co-operation and Development (OECD) was set up under a Convention signed in Paris on 14th December, 1960, which provides that the OECD shall promote policies designed:

- to achieve the highest sustainable economic growth and employment and a rising standard of living in Member countries, while maintaining financial stability, and thus to contribute to the development of the world economy;
- to contribute to sound economic expansion in Member as well as non-member countries in the process of economic development;
- to contribute to the expansion of world trade on a multilateral, non-discriminatory basis in accordance with international obligations.

The Members of OECD are Australia, Austria, Belgium, Canada, Denmark, Finland, France, the Federal Republic of Germany, Greece, Iceland, Ireland, Italy, Japan, Luxembourg, the Netherlands, New Zealand, Norway, Portugal, Spain, Sweden, Switzerland, Turkey, the United Kingdom and the United States.

* *

PREFACE

The development of national policies for education and employment has been a major concern of the OECD since the early 1960s. The approach taken in this work has been based on a clear recognition that while education and employment policies are distinct areas of government action they also have important common problems and objectives which need to be more clearly coordinated. This has become increasingly clear in recent years.

Knowledge is an essential resource in OECD economies, and one, unlike some other resources, can be renewed and developed. Consequently the creation, storage and diffusion of knowledge through education, and its utilisation in employment, are likely to be of growing importance in the economic development of OECD countries. Since many individuals spend a large part of their lives in education and work, policies in these two areas appreciably affect human welfare. Closer coordination between education and manpower policies may in addition be an essential condition of effectively reducing social disparities.

Following the Report of the Secretary-General's Group of Experts on Education and Working Life in Modern Society*, which made an initial review of problems and policy needs, the subject was taken up by governments. On the initiative of the OECD Committees on Education and Manpower and Social Affairs as well as the Governing Board of the Centre for Educational Research and Innovation, a Joint Working Party of officials from Member countries representing the interests of the two sides was set up to discuss and agree the objectives of public policies for education and working life and to consider how they can in practice be attained.

The report of the Working Party is published in the present volume. It begins with a summary of the main considerations and conclusions of the Joint Working Party. It lists the main guiding principles that are being adopted in Member countries to bring their policies for education and working life close together, and illustrates in each case the kinds of practical ways in which they can be implemented and which are in

*

OECD, 1975.

practice already being used. (Summary of main considerations and conclusions). Some of these principles represent significant changes in objectives in public policy. Better preparation in education for working life is now widely recognised as an important way of facilitating the transition to stable and satisfying employment, while there is a need for employment policies and practices to adapt to the rapidly changing educational characteristics of the labour force and its expectations.

The Report itself deals with two main sets of practical problems of current importance: the transition from education to working life, including the problems of the employment and unemployment of young people (Part III); and the ways in which the education and training of the labour force can better be utilised (Part IV). Finally, it discusses the main policy instruments that can be used by governments to strengthen the links between education and employment (Part V). The last section of Part V draws attention to the analysis and research that is needed to help improve the relevance, effectiveness and credibility of government policies in this field.

An Inventory of Innovative Measures by Member Countries in relation to the problems examined in the Report was also drawn up by the Working Party and will be published separately.

CONTENTS

3

SUMMARY OF MAIN CONSIDERATIONS
AND CONCLUSIONS

The Joint Working Party has focused its attention on two broad areas of policy: the transition from education to working life and the utilisation of education in employment. Consideration of the problems in these two areas suggests a number of conclusions about general policy objectives concerning education and working life, together with the main strategies and options which appear feasible.

Although they are of continuing, fundamental importance the issues considered in this report represent only part of the complex problems and interrelationships between education and working life. Because the problems and policy measures alike are undergoing rapid evolution, this present overall view of general policy objectives is necessarily preliminary and will need to be kept under review during the next few years. Nevertheless the findings of this report may be useful to Member governments in their efforts to introduce measures that form part of more clear and consistent forward-looking policies, especially where such measures are still relatively new and untested against experience.

For these reasons and also bearing in mind the widely differing conditions and plurality of interests in Member countries, it would be inappropriate to prescribe policies. Instead, the Joint Working Party has identified a number of common thematic conclusions. These conclusions take the form of broad objectives agreed by all Member countries which can be attained through different national strategies that combine the various possible types of measures according to national circumstances.

The joint roles of education and work

The basic objectives of extending opportunities for education and training and utilising them more fully throughout working life are to furnish essential resources for economic and social development, for cultural progress and individual well-being, and to help promote the most free exercise of choice about future forms of socio-economic development. Yet it is the view of the Joint Working Party that the potential of closer collaboration between policies for education and

5

work to contribute to economic production, social development and human welfare has yet to be fully realised in all Member countries (para. 6).

The joint Working Party concludes that governments and enterprises could give more attention in their long-term economic strategies to a recognition that knowledge, unlike many physical resources which are exhaustible and will become relatively more costly, is capable of continuous expansion and greater application. The joint Working Party emphasizes that the wide transmission of knowledge throughout the population and the labour force through formal and informal education and training will inevitably become more important, as a new world economic order emerges, in determining what Member countries can achieve, what they decide to achieve and the efficiency of economic production as well as the direction of social progress. To this end it is suggested that Member countries should give greater prominence to more co-ordinated policies for education and working life, with particular reference to looking for ways to improve the transition from education to working life and to utilise more fully throughout working life the rising levels of education and training of the labour force (paras. 7-18).

The adoption of these broad objectives has major implications for the development and co-ordination of both education and manpower policies which are discussed in the report. More particularly, it provides a long-term framework for dealing with the multitude of different problems thrown into prominence by the current and prospective employment situation and for giving an essential orientation to short-term measures. Action to deal with short-term problems, notably youth unemployment, will in fact be superficial if it is not firmly set in the context of longer-term objectives of renewing the labour force and making full use of its education. Similarly, the effectiveness of measures to develop employment in ways that improve personal, social, and cultural well-being will depend significantly on mobilising the education of the labour force throughout working life and recognising the profound influence that education is making on the values and expectations of the labour force. *

It should be noted that the broad objectives of bringing education and working life into a new relationship are closely related to those discussed under recurrent education. There is broad agreement that recurrent education can help develop new values in education and employment. It can have a revitalising effect on the labour force and increase its mobility. In the long run it will have important consequences for the organisation of work, the distribution of responsibility at the place of work and may affect the serenity of employment of the worker.

* See Recurrent Education: A Strategy for Life-Long Learning. OECD, CERI, 1972.

Overall policy co-ordination

Action in the fields of education and working life can be used simultaneously to promote individual, social and economic purposes. Recognising that responsibilities are shared among different levels and branches of government, enterprises, workers' organisations and other social institutions, there is a need in most Member countries to reinforce collaborative efforts among them.

To help create the essential conditions of more co-ordinated and consistent policy development, there is a need for overall strategies in Member countries which facilitate action to deal with specific problems according to agreed national policy objectives. To this end governments can:

i) develop national frameworks to identify issues and to agree basic objectives through formal or informal discussions with representatives of all interested bodies, especially of workers and employers (paras. 115 and 116);

ii) promote local collaborative action among all branches and levels of government, schools, enterprises, workers' representatives, voluntary bodies, etc. through various means such as enabling legislation, information, technical assistance, initial finance, etc. (para. 116);

iii) develop and maintain national and international arrangements to undertake research and experimentation, to exchange information and views about new policy initiatives and to assess measures (para. 143); and

iv) consider the collaborative arrangements needed to help create new orientations in public policies and programmes and in the allocation of resources, especially with a view to encouraging where possible a shift from income transfers towards more positive measures for training and employment creation (paras. 50, 51 and 142).

The co-responsibilities of governments and of other bodies

Evolving views about the complex mutual rights and duties that hold a society together are influencing the ways in which problems of education and working life are recognised and views about the responsibility of governments and other bodies for dealing with them. In some countries it is thought that the essential responsibility of governments is to help all individuals and institutions deal with these problems through the free exercise of their rights and duties. While policies are shaped at the national level within the framework of objectives agreed among the authorities concerned in consultation with employers' and workers' representatives, action is most effective if it is implemented with a minimum of direct government intervention at the local level. Others may take the view that education and employment are so vital to the community that governments have special responsibilities to exercise direct control and supervision over measures designed to further public policy objectives, such as minimum periods and levels of education and training, combinations of work and study, or the co-ordination of employment and training opportunities, particularly for young people.

Because in practice many students are unable to continue beyond compulsory education and take advantage of the upper secondary education that is usually provided at the expense of the state until the age of about 18, there is growing support in some countries for the idea that it may be desirable to recognise explicitly the entitlement of everyone to a certain number of years of free education and training beyond compulsory education (which at present is about eight to ten years in most Member countries), some of which can be taken up at any age, either in youth for upper secondary education or later in working life through recurrent education. Since those at work support those who are unable, for whatever reason, to be employed, the rights that have been recognised for an individual to be supported when he in turn is not employed can be adapted to take the form of additional opportunities for education and training, over and above a minimum entitlement. These opportunities may be related in a variety of ways to general employment conditions or to an individual's employment experience (para. 106).

Corresponding to the idea of the right to work and the duty to help support the community is the notion that the responsibility of the state is to ensure that all members of the labour force can acquire the basic competencies needed for entry into working life and continue to add to them. Behind this notion is the concept that if the community expects people to share the work that has to be done, it has an obligation to equip them to do so.

The Joint Working Party has identified a wide range of measures, including many recent imaginative innovations, which can be combined according to each country's objectives and circumstances in order to improve both general and specific preparation for employment for as many members of the labour force as possible. They include improvements in compulsory education (paras. 25-37); a new balance between general and vocational forms of education (paras. 42, 43, 47, 60-62) including improvements in curricula (paras. 25-29 and 83) and in the organisation of curricula (paras. 117-120); more opportunities for training during working life through educational leave from employment and recurrent education (paras. 102-106) and more opportunities for initial and further training that are better related to employment (paras. 121-131).

For the economy the entry of young people into working life is the most important single way by which the labour force is renewed and developed. The political responsibilities of governments towards young people are to facilitate this process as part of their policies towards the labour force as a whole, and at the same time to help young people obtain regular employment as part of overall social policy to create equitable opportunities for all age-groups. These responsibilities should be shared with all institutions in the community, notably schools and enterprises, families, teachers, employers, and unions and many voluntary bodies.

The education and employment of young people

To be realistic, measures to deal with the education and employment of young people should be firmly placed in the context of social and economic policies towards all age groups in the population and in the labour force, and also be designed to meet the different needs of young people which vary considerably according to their level of education and whether they are still in school or in the labour force.

For young people in education, there is a need in many cases to improve preparation for all aspects of adult life, including working life, especially of those groups which experience the greatest difficulty in making the transition to employment. Governments can devise long-term strategies to attain these objectives, by such means as:

i) improving basic education, through remedial teaching where needed, relating it more closely to everyday life and providing a better general knowledge of the world of work as an essential part of education (paras. 25-29);

ii) increasing the extent to which the teaching force has direct experience of the realities of work in other sectors of economic activity (paras. 34-37) ;

iii) improving opportunities for pupils to obtain first-hand experience of work as an essential part of their education (paras. 30-33);

iv) extending opportunities, encouragement and assistance to continue into and complete upper secondary education, either full-time or part-time (paras. 53-58);

v) reducing the pedagogical and social distinctions between general and vocational forms of education and by encouraging the development, in an experimental spirit, of a new balance between academic education and employment preparation at each level of education through a variety of combinations of general education, vocational preparation and work experience (paras. 31-33, 54, 55, 59-66);

vi) modifying assessment and credentialling practices and designing education certificates that better describe the content of studies followed and which give credit for employment and for training (para. 63).

Action to help young people entering the labour force make the transition into satisfactory working lives with possibilities of career development can serve the essential economic purpose of replenishing and extending the capacity of the labour force as well as minimising human and social costs. There is an economic as well as a social need to provide young people who enter the labour force before the age of 18 with personal assistance or support, which is comparable with the support given to those who remain at school (para. 57).

There is a need for an ensemble of measures which, in addition to providing better preparation for working life during education, aim to do so under general economic and employment conditions of all kinds by long-term strategy that includes:

i) clarifying the bases and principles on which education and employment counselling services are provided, and providing both services on a consistent basis (paras. 132-136);

ii) providing information and advice to employers about the education and training of the national and local labour force and about the competences of people with different levels of education and training (paras. 88 and 133);

iii) encouraging enterprises to develop more positive and explicit personnel policies consistent with the objectives of public manpower policies, and in particular by developing long-term recruiting and training policies, including induction training (paras. 42, 43, 91-97, 124) ;

iv) maintaining and where necessary extending long-term initial training opportunities, especially through apprenticesships or alternatively through employment in enterprises combined with training where apprenticeship is not suitable or possible (paras. 42 and 43);

v) action to identify the competences used in employment (paras. 83 and 84) and to provide the minimal competences through improvements in curricula in basic compulsory education and additional competences through more polyvalent kinds of curriculum organisation (para. 131).

A condition of developing such measures in realistic ways is to obtain a better knowledge and understanding, based on empirical investigations, of the values, attitudes and expectations of new entrants to the labour force and of employers where new entrants are concerned (para. 140).

The high level of <u>unemployment among young people</u> in Member countries is a serious problem which, because it has long-term as well as conjunctural origins, will be reduced but not eliminated by a return to higher levels of manpower utilisation. Action is therefore needed within the framework of the selective employment and manpower policies agreed by Member countries in the 1976 Recommendation on a General Employment and Manpower Policy for the labour force as a whole, and as part of a long-term strategy designed to maintain the renewal of the labour force and its adaptation to evolving patterns of employment. For taking the action urgently needed to deal with this problem governments can utilise the following types of measures:

    i) to help enterprises absorb school leavers more easily governments might consider reducing the concentration of school leaving at a single point of time during the year (para. 41);

    ii) Subsidies, which should usually be temporary, to help enterprises in the private sector recruit school leavers or unemployed young people, might preferably be offered for employment combined with training and wherever possible for long-term training. Programmes, which can be permanent, to provide subsidies need to be designed with care to avoid the substitution of young people for other workers and of temporary finance for other sources (paras. 44, 45 and 70);

    iii) when employment opportunities in the private sector are weak, temporary employment opportunities for young people can be created in public enterprises (paras. 50 and 51) and through government finance for community projects (para. 68), but these measures have also to meet the competing needs of other age groups.

There is a special need for measures to improve the employability of many young people who have the greatest difficulty in finding initial employment. This can be done by:

    i) special projects that associate various public and private bodies to provide combinations of initial employment experience, practical counselling and training (para. 47);

    ii) pre-apprenticeships (para. 42) ;

    iii) employing unemployed young people while adults are attending training courses (para. 46);

    iv) the creation of special jobs in the public sector (para. 50);

    v) subsidies for job creation in the private sector for unemployed school leavers.

Difficult problems of social priority towards different age groups, notably unemployed workers with family responsibilities and older and retired workers, may limit the extent to which employment opportunities can be created for young people under current and prospective economic conditions. The experimental measures being developed on a relatively small scale in several countries deserve to be more widely known and can be extended as experience of them is assessed and resources can be released. Bearing in mind these practical limits there is considerable scope for new initiatives to extend training for young people. Employment can be increased by subsidies within public expenditure constraints since gross public outlays are offset by increased revenues and savings on social security payments. The long-term development of the productive capacity of the labour force is an argument for the degree of priority that can be given to young people.

More balanced policies for education and employment

There is a need for a better balance between policies for education and working life. The action being taken in all countries to raise levels of education and training will inevitably lead to greater under-utilisation of manpower and personal frustration if it is not complemented by action to create a sufficient number and type of employment opportunities. It will be increasingly in the interests of enterprises to do so in order to obtain personnel and improve competitive efficiency. If minimum levels of education and training are to be provided as a right, it will be necessary to recognise that failing to provide opportunities to use such education and training entails considerable economic waste and personal frustration. Moreover, the burden of adaptation cannot be placed on individuals alone. With rising levels of education in the labour force it is inevitable that there should be an increasing reciprocal adaptation of economies to individual abilities and desires. It is recognised that there are limits to long-term growth and to the extent to which the level and composition of aggregate demand can in the short term be modified to create employment. Special importance, therefore, attaches to the consideration that is being given to more widespread applications of selective employment and manpower policies to increase employment at any given level of aggregate demand, and to reduce the extent to which employment is simply treated as a demand derived from short-term production considerations, in ways that recognise that education and training are vital dimensions of the labour force.

To this end countries might consider policy strategies that aim to create and develop:

i)   education for working life as a vital part of preparation for life as a whole with a view to enabling individuals to exercise sound judgment about it as well as engage in it (paras. 25-27, 59-62, 64-66 and 83);

ii)   enterprise manpower policies more oriented towards the continuing development of individuals and the full use of their skills, efforts and interests (paras. 91-101) ;

iii) conditions under which all levels of government employers and workers' representatives and working bodies collaborate in new ways to resolve problems (paras. 71 and 72);

iv) wider arrangements for leave of absence for education and training (paras. 102-106);

v)   easier transition for young new entrants and re-entrants to the labour force (paras. 79-84);

vi)   more part-time opportunities for education and employment (para. 54); and

vii)   training by enterprises (paras. 128-129).

Greater versatility and mobility of individuals

A key objective should be to promote an environment in which individuals can be more versatile and more mobile during their working lives. While aiming to make education generally more relevant to working life it is nevertheless highly desirable to devise forms of education and employment which permit the development of less rigid linkages between specific educational preparation and qualifications on one hand and specific levels of entry to employment or careers on the other. To this end, education and training systems could better be adapted to meet the learning needs of students of all ages, to prepare them more effectively for entry to and movement through working life, and ensure the full expansion of the skills, abilities and interests of the labour force. Enterprises, in order continuously to increase their capacity and productivity, need to adapt the organisation of work and the content of jobs with a view to creating dynamic employment and career possibilities and a quality of working life better able to satisfy a more educated labour force.

These objectives can be attained through strategies which combine action designed to:

i)   develop more polyvalent curricula (paras. 83, 117-120);

ii)   relate training to new concepts of work functions that replace the traditional concept of occupation (para. 131);

iii)   give full or partial credit in education and training for practical experience and employment (para. 63);

iv)   make credits interchangeable among all kinds of education and training institutions within a country, including training in enterprises;

v)   extend opportunities to combine classroom instruction and practical experience, including employment (paras. 30-32, 43, 54, 62, 64-66 and 82);

vi)   make credentials more relevant to employment (para. 63);

vii)   promote better recruiting and selection methods by enterprises related to previous employment experiences and personal potential as well as education and training (paras. 89-90);

viii)   encourage more flexible employment patterns and possibilities within enterprises (paras. 91-93, 102-106) ;

ix)   encourage arrangements for participation or consultation within enterprises (paras. 98-101).

More equitable life-time opportunities

Recognition of the objective of creating more equitable life-time opportunities is a condition of action to help overcome the powerful forces of social selection that arise in both education and working life and which cannot effectively be reduced by education or manpower policies alone.   This objective is important for its own sake especially if, when policies are being formulated, the needs of those who suffer the more extreme forms of disadvantage are borne in mind.

A concerted strategy for attaining this objective can be developed in the course of designing the measures that governments take to:

i) improve basic compulsory education in order to provide an understanding of working life as part of initial preparation for entry into it (paras. 26-39);

ii) extend remedial teaching (para. 25);

iii) encourage more students to remain in and complete upper seondary education (paras. 53 58);

iv) develop better counselling, placement and training for those who leave early (paras. 56 and 132-136);

v) provide a minimum of essential vocational preparation either in school or in enterprises that will enable all new entrants to begin work (paras. 123-124);

vi) extend arrangements for paid educational leave and facilities for recurrent education (paras. 102-106);

vii) encourage enterprises to train adults according to their needs and learning capacities and the broader needs of the economy as well as those of the enterprise (paras. 128-129);

viii) develop new means to combine temporary job creation counselling and training for unemployed young people, especially those who have experienced difficulty in school (paras. 47-49) ;

ix) consider making explicit the right to a minimum number of years of free education beyond compulsory schooling, some of which can be taken at any age with additional rights related to employment (paras. 53, 54, 57 and 106);

x) consider the design of financial arrangements that can enable individuals to choose freely how to organise their lives among education, work and leisure, including the possibility of additional temporary finance for the constructive use of time during unemployment (paras. 58, 69, 70, 106 and 142).

I

INTRODUCTION: SCOPE OF THE REPORT

1. The Joint Working Party, after an initial exploratory discussion, agreed that since the field of concern is large, complex and has received relatively little attention, its work should be confined to a limited number of important questions. It was agreed that the questions chosen for consideration should be those which call for action by both the education and manpower authorities, either through parallel efforts directed towards common objectives or through collaboration between them.

2. More particularly it was agreed that the work should focus on a number of problems under two issues of fundamental importance: the transition from education to working life, and the development and utilisation of the education of the labour force during working life. The Joint Working Party recognises that there are many issues of concern to education and manpower policies respectively which are beyond the scope of this report, many of which are being examined under other activities of the Education and the Manpower and Social Affairs Committees and the Centre for Educational Research and Innovation.* The measures considered by the Joint Working Party are not intended to be the chief means of dealing with other major problems that are primarily the concern of policies for education and employment respectively, although they may have a limited effect on them.

3. This report :

   i)   briefly outlines the main issues on which the Joint Working Party decided to concentrate (Part II);

   ii) examines these problems with a view to identifying the types of action that are being taken by governments to deal with them (Parts III and IV); and

   iii discusses the main policy instruments that can be used by governments to help bring education and working life close together.

---

*   For example on Employment, Migration, the Role of Women in the Economy, Recurrent Education, Learning Opportunities for Adults, Admission Policies in Post-secondary Education, etc.

4.   While the scope of this examination is limited the Joint Working Party suggests the general objectives that might be pursued by governments in attempting to develop and co-ordinate their policies for education and working life; together with the guiding principles for the use of the main policy instruments that are relevant; and in doing so indicates the kinds of practical measures that can be and are being used by governments in their national strategies. (Summary of main considerations and conclusions).

II

SELECTED MAJOR ISSUES

5.   The acquisition of knowledge and skills through formal and informal education and training, and their application through employment
are two of the basic factors in the evolution of production and wealth in
OECD countries.   In addition, education and employment, which together absorb a significant part of human life, heavily influence the
patterns of behaviour, opportunity and welfare of most citizens.   Yet
in recent years the role of education as a factor in economic growth
has been questioned.   Furthermore, although the worlds of education
and work are distinct, the responsibilities for public policies towards
them have come to be shared amongst different ministries and levels
of government.

6.   The potential of education and work to contribute to economic
production, social development and human welfare has yet to be fully
realised.   Considerable progress towards this fundamental objective
could be made if governments would give priority attention to problems
arising in two main areas of current and continuing importance, which
exist in all countries regardless of national education and economic
systems of particular conjunctural situations:

  i)   improving the transition from education to working life; and
  ii)   improving the utilisation of the education and training of the
        labour force during working life.

A.   TRENDS AND PROSPECTS IN THE ECONOMY,
IN EMPLOYMENT AND IN EDUCATION

7.   The view that is taken of these issues and the policies that are
applied will be most realistic if they are placed in the context of the
realities of the current and prospective socio-economic situation of the
OECD area.   In this connection three main time-horizons can usefully
be taken into account.

  i)   The short term

      The OECD area is recovering from a recession that has been
more extensive, deeper and longer than any other during the postwar

years. The nature of the problems of education and working life has been changing rapidly as the employment situation evolves. In most countries levels of manpower utilisation have fallen since 1973; recorded unemployment is at high rates, and increasing in duration; underemployment, indicated by reductions in productivity, has risen; and in several countries total employment actually fell in 1974 and 1975, which is unusual, and shows little sign of rapid recovery. In most OECD countries it is a well-established objective to encourage contra-cyclical increases in training; and trends in enrolments may have been influenced further in that direction by individual decisions to prolong general education or to seek training.

ii) The medium term

The economies of OECD countries, which are continuously transformed by the growth of consumption, production and technical change, are being further altered by the major changes since 1972 in the economic relationships between the OECD area and the rest of the world. In most countries medium-term prospects for expenditures on formal education are that their rapid growth since the early 1960s will not be sustained at the same rate, although education services will continue to evolve to meet new needs and objectives and demographic changes. Expenditures on training may rise: several governments have announced planned increases for the next few years. However, where training is financed by payroll taxes any expansion is likely to be slow. Most OECD countries, which hitherto had experienced a period of overall scarcity of manpower during the rapid growth of most of the postwar period, have now entered a phase of prospectively lower levels of manpower utilisation. Since its inception the aims of the Organisation have included achieving the highest sustainable economic growth and employment. Following the meeting of the Manpower and Social Affairs Committee at Ministerial level in March 1976 the Council of the Organisation adopted a Recommendation on a General Employment and Manpower policy in which "OECD countries re-affirm their commitment to full employment as a goal of policy".* Nevertheless, the economic situation and prospects in the OECD area are such that, in most countries, the moderate rate of recovery in output is expected to absorb unemployment more slowly than in previous upturns and to make future patterns of employment more uncertain than usual in times of recovery.

iii) The long term

There is even greater uncertainty about the form that socio-economic development will take in the more distant future under the

---

*   See the Recommendation PRESS/A(76)9.

18

influence of endogenous changes or how far its direction can be changed by public policy. Awareness of the growing economic, human and environmental costs of growth has created a need and a willingness to explore the possibilities of a more positive social policy. It must be anticipated that the penetration of the labour force by an increasing proportion of more highly educated citizens will have profound influences on the capacity of OECD economies, on expectations and on human and political relations at work.

B. THE TRANSITION FROM EDUCATION
TO WORKING LIFE

8. For the economy the movement of young people into working life is the most important single way in which the labour force and its average level of education is renewed and developed. The same is true for the personnel of most enterprises. Yet there is growing agreement that for a large proportion of young people, preparation for working life is inadequate and that the transition to working life is often unnecessarily difficult and slow, particularly for low socio-economic categories and for women. This is further compounded by the views that many young people hold about the unsatisfactory nature of work opportunities that the economy offers.

9. Employers are often reluctant to employ young people because many of them lack appropriate vocational skill and employment experience. In some employers' views, some young people do not possess the basic skills of literacy, numeracy and communication, or the personal qualities that many employers prefer. The initial contribution of new entrants to production is often low, and even negative. During favourable economic conditions some employers may be prepared to accept these costs as part of the total cost of renewing their personnel, but others prefer older workers or women returning to the labour force who are already trained or more likely to work regularly. When they do employ young people, employers often engage in a search, that is not always successful, for people with specific skills or the ability to adapt to the circumstances of the enterprise. Some enterprises do not provide training, including induction, if they are not convinced of the usefulness of it or if they fear that, in periods of relatively high employment, they may lose the personnel they have trained.

10. For the age group as a whole and for many individuals within it, the transition from education to firm establishment in working life takes several years. Boys and girls complain that they are often inadequately or wrongly prepared in school and that counselling is not

satisfactory. There is a marked seasonal pattern in unemployment while school leavers are absorbed into employment. Once in employment, opportunities during working life to acquire experience, education and training, responsibility and income are often limited by traditional employment structures and practices and by the absence of facilities for further education and training.

11. Although relatively little is known in detail about the problems of transition, which are obviously different for each individual, it seems clear that they vary significantly among different age-groups and types and levels of education and training.

12. These difficulties during the transition impose opportunity costs: individuals lose income and work satisfaction, employers and the economy lose production both currently and in the future, as well as the outlays on recruitment. While part of the high rates of turnover among young people performs the useful role of allocating the labour force among employers and jobs, part of it entails waste in the form of loss of output and is one of the sources of inflationary pressure.

13. In the current recession the costs have fallen heavily on young people. In many countries the arrival in the labour force of a large cohort of boys and girls leaving school, especially after compulsory education, has coincided with a stagnation or even a fall in the level of employment. National rates of unemployment among young people have ranged up to 20 per cent in some Member countries, and double that figure in some regions or among certain categories of them. For many young people their first experience of life in the labour force is unemployment; and it is now increasing in duration, although not necessarily more than among older workers. In these circumstances pressures on liquidity among enterprises have not only denied many young people an initial work experience, they have also reduced training opportunities, especially long-term ones such as apprenticeship.

14. More particularly, there is growing concern for the categories of young people, upon whom these costs fall most heavily of all because they are especially vulnerable. The transition to an employment corresponding to their qualifications, expectations and aspirations, either in the first job or later, which is difficult and frustrating at all levels of education, may be particularly protracted and entail more broken employment and unemployment among the young school leavers with lower levels of education and no training. There are many young people, often from families whose socio-economic status is low, who experience problems at school, including difficulty in learning, who leave school early without either formal qualifications or vocational skills, who experience corresponding difficulties in obtaining an initial job or stable employment with opportunities to obtain training, more

than a very low income, or the prospect of subsequent personal development during working life. Moreover once in types of employment that are low level or unstable, or both, they tend to be considered suitable only for that type of work.

C. THE DEVELOPMENT AND UTILISATION OF THE EDUCATION AND TRAINING OF THE LABOUR FORCE DURING WORKING LIFE

15. The great expansion of education in Member countries since the early 1960s, which accompanied their economic growth, has significantly increased the proportion of people in the labour force with extended education and high levels of educational attainment. In some countries, such as Australia and Canada, immigration has further raised the average level of education in the labour force. The expansion of education has raised the expectations and aspirations of many individuals for jobs and careers in which they can use their education and find wider opportunities for personal satisfaction and development. Yet the overall structure of employment in the economy and the content of most jobs do not correspond to these higher levels of educational attainment and raised aspirations. There are signs of a long-term increase in the under-utilisation of manpower which is partly indicated by a rise in the level of unemployment from one recession to another since the early 1960s. Under-utilisation also takes the form of a failure to provide the kinds of jobs that are related to individual abilities. There remains a high proportion of jobs that are dirty, dangerous, boring, entail low skills, are low in pay or status or offer no possibilities for development, many of which do not attract members of the domestic labour force even when unemployment is high.

16. In addition, opportunities to utilise the rising educational levels of the labour force have been limited by the serious check to the rate of growth in employment and fixed capital that has occurred in most Member countries during the last two or three years.

17. This problem could well be aggravated in the future. The average level of educational attainment of the labour force will be further raised by the death and retirement of the older age groups of the labour force whose average levels of education are relatively low. The total "stock" of skills and abilities will also continue to be raised by the cumulative effects of improvements in the quality and dispersion of education, the training programmes carried out each year, and the expansion of education for adults as arrangements for educational leave and recurrent education become more widespread and effective. The changes in immigration of more educated workers into countries such as Australia

and Canada and of less well-educated foreign workers into European
Member countries, will no doubt affect the patterns of education
and skills of their labour forces in ways that are hard to anticipate.

18.   In the light of these considerations there is a need to devise
more co-ordinated means by which policies for both education and
working life can be directed towards the better development of
individuals and the utilisation of their education and training in employment, especially so that young people entering working life can
contribute as fully as possible to social and economic development
Rather than considering education as the "residual factor" in economic
development, it seems necessary to affirm that in the long run it is
a major factor determining the social, economic and broader cultural
development of our societies.   In view of increasing financial constraints,
there is a need in many cases to improve the management of education.
In this long-term perspective there is a complementary need to find
ways of adapting the organisation and content of employment opportunities
in order to utilise more fully the rising levels of educational attainment
and the skills and abilities of the labour force.   The aim here is to
improve productivity and competitive efficiency as well as personal
income and satisfaction in work.   Such an approach is one of the basic
conditions of the successful development of policies to raise the level
of employment at given levels of aggregate demand pressure, as part
of the selective employment and manpower measures contained in the
1976 Recommendation of a General Employment and Manpower Policy.
There is a challenge to find operational ways of doing so.

D.   SHARED RESPONSIBILITIES AND THEIR CO-ORDINATION

19.   The responsibilities for dealing with these problems are shared
among many jurisdictions : among the public authorities, notably
between the education and manpower authorities; and also among
different branches and levels of government, unions, employers and
many other voluntary agencies.   The problem that has to be faced
in bringing policies into a closer and more consistent focus, is how
to encourage the practitioners in the various governmental and non-
governmental bodies to become more sensitive and responsive to the
need to devise the practical action that has to be taken; when jurisdictions are shared there is a danger of unhealthy competitiveness
and recrimination; so that if effective solutions are to be found, ways
have to be found to deal with problems on a shared, collaborative
basis.

III

THE TRANSITION FROM EDUCATION
TO WORKING LIFE

A. THE MAIN LEVELS OF EDUCATION

20. The problems of the transition to working life vary considerably according to each level of education and training and call for different emphases in policies and combinations of measures towards preparation within each level and subsequent entry into working life. Nevertheless it will be seen that there are common elements which make it possible to propose some common objectives.

21. In most Member countries it is possible to identify and consider these problems by reference to three main levels of education: compulsory basic schooling (consisting of primary and lower secondary); upper secondary; and higher education (short-cycle, degree level and post-graduate cycles). Within each level account has to be taken of the different types of study.

22. The balance among these main levels and sectors of education is undergoing major changes as a result of policies directed towards the expansion of upper secondary education and the limitation of certain types of higher education. This will lead to significant changes in the flows of young people moving from each level of education into the labour force. It will in turn generate corresponding changes in the composition of each age-cohort according to level of education. There will be further changes as a result of the diversification that is taking place within each level of education. These flows are progressively changing the educational characteristics of the labour force.

23. The age at which each level of education is completed does not correspond closely, if at all, with the ages at which people move into the labour force. In most Member countries children are, with few exceptions, in full-time compulsory education until the age of 14 to 16, which enables them to complete the primary and lower secondary cycles and some of them to begin the upper secondary cycle. At the age of 15 most young people are still in school. The years from 16 to 19 are those when most of them move into the labour force, so that by age 19 only some 20 per cent or less of an age cohort is left in full-time higher education.

24. In some countries there are significant differences among the minimum legal ages at which young people can leave school, be employed, receive training under public training programmes or be entitled to unemployment benefits. The harmonisation of these arrangements would help ease the transition from school to normal working-life.

B. COMPULSORY FULL-TIME EDUCATION

1. Preparation during compulsory education

25. A major objective of compulsory education is to provide a common, basic learning experience for all pupils which will prepare them for everyday life, including subsequently highly diversified patterns of education and employment. The need for the wide application of compensatory measures and individualised teaching to make up for inadequacies in school performance is generally recognised, if not always effectively applied. Different views persist, however, about when, during the years of compulsory education, preparation for working life can and should be provided and what forms it can best take. To this end the following main possible types of action merit consideration.

i) Action to improve curriculum

26. Preparation for working life during compulsory schooling has a different purpose from preparation during other levels of education. It can most usefully be directed towards providing an initial knowledge of the economy and of the world of work at all stages, especially if managers, union leaders and other people with direct knowledge of working life are concerned. It can become progressively more detailed, conferring an awareness of the role of work in society and in each pupil's future life, and an initial basis for the realistic exercise of choices through life. Ideally these choices would reflect personal interests and abilities as well as the employment opportunities that arise.

.27. One realisation of this objective is illustrated by the concept of career education which has spread through the United States during the last five years. The concept is implemented flexibly through such means as instruction, work experience and counselling, or combinations of them. By 1975 forty-two states had formal policies on career education, and twenty-eight had full-time staff coordinators. At the local level about half of all students were in school districts where it was substantially implemented. Under the concept of career education instruction is given by individuals from enterprises, workers' organisations and governments, and about 45 per cent of the districts give credit for work outside the school. Initial assessments indicate that it improves students' motivations, especially the children of parents with little education and that it opens additional avenues of career exploration beyond those followed by the family and by neighbours.

28. In many countries, curricula now include studies in such things as citizenship, driver education and sex education, with a view to preparing students for their various roles in adult life. Yet, although all individuals either work or depend on others at work, relatively few curricula include an introduction to the economy, the nature of enterprises, the role of unions and other background knowledge about working life. This gap has been filled in Germany, where the curriculum now includes studies of the world of work (Arbeitslehre).

29. In several countries, especially where attempts are made to "stream" those in compulsory education according to different types of ability, some specific vocational preparation begins at the relatively early age of about 11 to 13. This presents parents with difficult problems of choice which cannot easily be corrected during later school years or after the child has left school. There are social as well as pedagogic reasons for thinking that sharp differentiation at this age is premature, a view which has been reflected in the spread of the comprehensive principle in compulsory education. The need for a common educational experience for all children and, it has been suggested, the changes which occur during adolescence in behaviour, interest and the ability to learn abstract ideas and to reason, point to the desirability of deferring major choice in curricula until the end of early adolescence, when children become more consciously interested in social problems and in their own future, and their potential development can be more easily assessed.* It is thus more realistic to delay the provision of specific vocational instruction and counselling to the age of about 15 or later, and to aim during compulsory education to provide a basis for subsequent vocational training.

ii) The provision of work experience during compulsory education

30. Initiatives to help pupils in compulsory education learn about employment tend to be limited to the traditional practice of visits to enterprises and visits by employers. There is scope to improve the latter by, for example, providing opportunities for workers' representatives or apprentices to participate and also by relating such initiatives more closely to the curriculum.

31. However, periods of work experience for pupils in compulsory education could have a strong influence on their awareness of the

---

*   See Compulsory Secondary Education, OECD/CERI (to be published).

realities of working life and their choice of employment, careers, further education and training. Moreover, experience also suggests that periods of work can be designed to provide an authentic educational experience if they are fully integrated into the curriculum. It follows that academic credit for such periods should be accorded.

32. At present there are relatively few suitable opportunities for this purpose. They are sometimes scarce in rural areas, although in Portugal a few schools have developed schemes to grow and sell agricultural products. It is in the collective interest of employers that many of them should provide work experience. The resolution of such questions as the cost to enterprises, wages, insurance and other matters relating to employment of young people will depend, of course, on particular situations and arrangements in the various countries. It is in the interests of pupils and enterprises that such opportunities should be available to pupils of all levels of ability; and care should be taken to ensure that they are not confined to weaker or difficult pupils.

33. The possibilities of developing a variety of new local approaches are illustrated by the Work/Education initiative in the United States, introduced in 1976 as a co-operative project of the Departments of Labor, Commerce and Health, Education and Welfare. The National Alliance of Businessmen, the American Association of Community and Junior Colleges and the National Manpower Institute have received grants of U.S. $ 1.8 million to establish education/work councils and to co-ordinate resources in up to 32 communities. These approaches will include work experience in some communities, but will use different techniques in others.

     iii)   Teachers' experience of working life outside the education sector

34. Some of the divergence between education and working life could be reduced significantly if more teachers had experience of employment in other sectors. This is partly a matter for initial as well as in-service training. Some school authorities already prefer teachers who have had other kinds of employment before or after their training as teachers and in a number of cases some curricula in teachers' training have been modified; but it is striking that opportunities for teachers to acquire other employment experience during their years of service do not generally appear to exist; and at present limited employment opportunities outside education are inhibiting some of the mobility from teaching that normally takes place.

35. The acquisition by teachers of experience in other occupations and industries could be facilitated by governments in several ways. In addition, several approaches could be discussed with teachers' representatives, such as the possibility of paying special allowances

comparable with those given in some countries for additional academic qualifications, or leave without pay for a sabbatical year or two without loss of seniority in teaching. There are also opportunities for both new graduates and experienced teachers to work in the field of aid to developing countries and obtain experience of international problems.

36. Yet another possibility is to use the facilities of recurrent education. Fo example, in Sweden teachers of vocational subjects have long been entitled to leave of absence for employment related to their teaching. From July 1977 the entitlement to fully paid leave of absence for two to four weeks will be extended to enable all teachers in compulsory and upper secondary schools to observe or engage in gainful employment in other industries. In 1977 about 200 teachers are expected to benefit.

37. Finally, an experiment was undertaken in France where on the initiative of the Ministry of National Education arrangements were made for teachers from various disciplines in general and technical education to be released for the entire school year for a training assignment in an enterprise. It was suggested however that because employment was arranged by negotiation between school administrators and the employers' associations, the teachers were cut off from other workers and from trade unions and so were not fully exposed to the realities of normal employment. This project has been discontinued for lack of funds.

38. In a reciprocal way it is equally important to take positive steps to bring other people into the teaching force from outside it as a way of enriching its experience. The experience of many people in employment, such as industrialists, union leaders and managers, is virtually unused in teaching and could be made available through occasional and part-time teaching as well as through full-time work. There is a tradition of part-time teaching in several countries in technical institutions which merits consideration in the case of teachers in general education. It is however important to stress that all teachers should be properly trained.

39. To these ends the public employment services have a role to play. They might encourage or help to initiate arrangements that permit teachers to obtain experience in enterprises as well as help school authorities recruit former teachers who have worked in other fields. They can also make known opportunities for training as teachers for adults with employment histories outside education.

2. Entry into the labour force from compulsory education

40. For many young people who go into the labour force at the end of compulsory education, the central problem is that, because of their youth and lack of specific training and experience, they are among the

least well-equipped to compete for jobs, especially the more attractive ones. Because these young people can often only obtain a first job in occupations or industries where turnover is high and jobs are unstable they begin to acquire broken employment histories.which in practice act as barriers to access to better types of employment. Since the life-time chances of people who do not transfer into upper secondary education are often seriously restricted, the right to recurrent education opportunities later in life is an important means of helping equalise opportunities for both learning and employment.*   In the short-term, the burden on them and on the community can be considerably eased by a variety of measures which governments are beginning to develop to create employment and training opportunities.

i)   The time of leaving school

41.   School leaving tends to be concentrated at two or three points during the calendar year, but the absorption of the cohort of school leavers into employment is spread over several months during which time many young people obtain their first experience of life in the labour force in the form of unemployment. The problem has become considerably aggravated by the rising long-term trend in unemployment as well as by the recession and the changes in demographic structure. While employers could more easily absorb a more regular flow of school leavers throughout the year, there are practical obstacles and resistances to changes in the time of leaving school, and few major initiatives appear to have been taken to resolve this problem. One exception is the United Kingdom, where it is now possible for some pupils to leave at the end of May instead of June.   Another is the United States, where about 140 school districts have implemented a year-round schedule of school attendance at the elementary and secondary levels and where other districts are considering doing the same. In view of the very large numbers involved, it should be possible to explore the possibilities of spreading the course given at present during the final school year over a period of more than a year and combining it with initial employment projects, with a view to permitting a more even flow to the labour force and allowing pupils to complete their course.   It has also been suggested that staggered vacations by enterprises could help absorb some school leavers.

ii)   Apprenticeship

42.   Many pupils leaving compulsory education enter traditional apprenticeships, although their relative importance varies greatly among countries.   Even in countries such as Germany where the

---

*   See Recurrent Education: a strategy for life-long learning, (CERI, 1972) and Recurrent Education: trends and issues, (CERI, 1975).

majority of young people receive an apprenticeship training, there is
a need to review traditional apprenticeship schemes with a view to
increasing the availability of skilled manpower, improving the quality
of training, diminishing their social selectivity, shortening the duration
of training, facilitating transfers to further education, and promoting
mobility in employment. In view of the current decline in the number
of new apprenticeships, there is a special need for action by governments to maintain or even increase the future availability of qualified
manpower by encouraging and helping enterprises continue to train a
sufficient number of apprentices. An example is the initiative of the
Australian authorities in 1975 to give increased subsidies to enterprises that would maintain or increase their apprenticeships. This
was replaced in 1977 by a completely new scheme of financial support
for apprenticeship. Some countries, such as Ireland, are introducing
off-the-job training in the first year. Such measures are based on a
recognition that apprenticeship is a major long-term alternative to
temporary employment creation and short-term training. In some
countries the number of entrants could be increased if the minimum
age limits were made more flexible. Extended arrangements for
pre-apprenticeships could be considered as a means of helping some
young people, especially those who are educationally and socially
disadvantaged, qualify for entry to apprenticeship and choose a career
as a skilled craftsman. Governments, enterprises and workers'
representatives could also consider extending the range of occupations
for which apprenticeship is available, and devising other combinations
of classroom instruction and practical experience.

iii) Other combinations of employment and training

43. For school leavers who do not take an apprenticeship, possibly
because they have not made the decision in time, and who have difficulty
in obtaining work, it is desirable to create other opportunities for initial
employment that includes training. A measure which helps do so in a
way that also recognises the financial difficulties of enterprises is the
employment-training contract in France. Moreover, this measure
enables enterprises to provide either short-term training for a job
within the enterprise or longer-term training for an occupational
qualification. The minimum age-limits are set in such a way that
these contracts supplement and do not compete with normal apprenticeships.

iv) Employment and training subsidies

44. Recognising the difficulties of many enterprises, especially in
present conditions, of meeting the costs of hiring and training school
leavers, there is scope for the wider use of financial assistance and
incentives to employers in the private sector. In view of the increasing
duration of unemployment in the current recession, the effectiveness

of such measures depends in part on their being correctly focused on the appropriate part of the labour force. An illustration is the replacement in the United Kingdom of the temporary recruitment subsidy for school leavers, which was in force from October 1975 to September 1976, by a subsidy for unemployed young people. In Norway, financial help was made available in 1975 and 1976 to help private enterprises provide temporary employment or three months' training for unemployed young people.

45.   The appropriateness and effectiveness of subsidies is however a complex question about which views differ among countries and within them. On one hand they can help create more equitable opportunities. On the other hand there is a special need in using such techniques to avoid the substitution of temporary public financing for other financial sources instead of supplementing them, and at the same time to avoid the substitution of unemployed young people for other employed workers instead of increasing employment and training. Thus the criteria of eligibility have to be defined with care. Bearing in mind the need to help create temporary employment for workers of all ages there is a limit to the extent to which governments can finance such measures for young people. Thus these types of measures may remain small in scale compared with the total number of school leavers entering the labour force, or even current increases in them.

v)   Replacements for older workers in training

46.   Interesting variants of subsidies are the Swedish measures to provide either permanent or temporary employment for unemployed young people who replace permanent employees who are taking training. An initial assessment of these measures suggests that even temporary employment can help improve the employability of those concerned, as well as helping them become more aware of employment conditions and prospects. Since 1973 about 7,000 young people have been employed temporarily to replace about 14,000 public employees in training.

vi)   Aid to young people who experience special difficulties

47.   The seriousness and complexity of the problems that young people have to face in making an effective transition to working life calls for action, preferably in collaboration, by all social institutions. Growing experience suggests that there are many public and voluntary bodies each of which has its own contribution to make to identifying young people in need and helping solve their multiple problems. For example, in the United Kingdom the Community Industry Scheme for young people aged from 16-18 who have greater difficulty than others in obtaining and keeping a job, aims to help them overcome personal problems, cope better with life in society, contribute to the community and prepare for regular employment. It is jointly managed by a

voluntary body, a government department and the social partners, financed by the central government with material help from local governments, and activities are supervised by a leader who is usually a skilled tradesman. Up to 5,500 places have been authorised; and more than 11,000 young people have been employed, of whom about half entered full-time employment.

48.　In 1976 the British Government launched a programme of pilot schemes of unified vocational preparation for young people aged 16 to 19 who leave school and go into jobs with little or no further education or training. Some unemployed school leavers are also taking part. The programme is jointly designed and administered by the Department of Education and Science, the Department of Employment and the Training Services Agency. It is intended eventually to serve about 6,000 young people a year and be financed within existing planned total expenditure. Another example is that of Project 70,001 Ltd., in the United States in the field of retail sales and distribution which serves some 2,000 to 2,500 young people.

49.　The novelty of such initiatives lies partly in collaboration among governments and other agencies, and partly in the fact that employment is combined with some training and also with career or employment counselling.

vii)　Temporary public employment creation

50.　While the private sector of the economy has been unable to generate a sufficient total number of jobs, even with special assistance, governments have been able to some extent to create temporary employment in the public sector. While this is intended to help all types of unemployed workers, on the principle contained in the 1976 Recommendation on a General Employment and Manpower Policy that it is better to pay people to be gainfully occupied than remain unemployed, such measures have a special importance for young people if they can help them obtain their first job. It is desirable that, where feasible, resources should be used to promote employment rather than for income transfers. This approach has been used in the United States and was significantly extended during the 1974/75 recession.

51.　To help ensure that the unemployed benefit, it may be essential to provide initial training for the temporary work and subsequent training for permanent employment. The constraints on government expenditures and other resistances to increasing the size of the public sector may limit the extent to which this approach can be used in several countries. When finance for temporary job creation is withdrawn as the rate of unemployment falls other measures are needed to deal with young people who remain unemployed in more normal employment conditions. Particular care is needed to ensure that such measures do not act as disincentives to education or ordinary employment.

C.   UPPER SECONDARY EDUCATION

52.   The years of upper secondary education are crucial to the economic and social objectives of both education and manpower policies.
One reason is that it is possible to offer a more complete preparation
for working life and other social roles than is possible during compulsory
education, the latter part of which largely coincides with puberty and
early adolescence.   The other is that it is the stage of education and
training at which social selection through access to opportunities for
education and employment becomes most clearly manifest.

1.   Participation in upper secondary education

53.   The voluntary extension of education.   The life-time chances of
most people can significantly be increased if they continue into and
complete upper secondary education.   Many countries aim to make
available facilities for some form of education and training until the
age of 18* as a mater of public responsibility.   The advocates of
extending education beyond the current compulsory school leaving age
limit of 15/16, which applies in most Member countries, argue that the
school is the social institution best able to take care of the development
of all young people until the age of legal maturity.   However, while
most countries subscribe to the need for some form of education and/
or training for all people up to 18, they nearly all seek to achieve this
on a voluntary basis, including encouragement to remain in school or
in a combination of school and working experience.   It may be appropriate to give many young people who would otherwise be unemployed
the opportunity to prolong their education.   It is, however, desirable
to do so with care because it can create boredom for many students
who remain in school (which has come to be known as a "drag-out"
problem that is as undesirable as "drop-out").   Moreover, it can
postpone and even aggravate employment difficulties.

54.   Compulsory part-time education and training.   A significant
option in extending compulsory education is to require part-time
attendance.   In Germany, when compulsory full-time education ends
after nine years at age 15, compulsory part-time school continues, as
a rule for another three years.   Anyone who does not continue voluntary
secondary education must attend a vocational school part-time.   In the
Netherlands the employment of students in compulsory part-time education was stimulated in 1976 by the payment of a premium of Dfl. 50
a week to employers.   A more general proposition, which is the subject

---

*   The corresponding age is lower in some less-developed Member countries.

of continuing debate in that country, is to make some form of education compulsory for everybody until the age of 18. This is part of proposals for a completely new system of education in the Netherlands.*

55. Other forms of obligation to continue part-time education. In countries where apprenticeship is practised, there is a requirement that trainees in specified occupations should attend further part-time education which, although agreed by employers' and workers' representatives, is ultimately sanctioned by legislation requiring certification after examination. As economies and technologies evolve and new types of work or occupations emerge, it may be appropriate to consider whether formal apprenticeship or other similar combinations of instruction and practical experience should not be extended to them. This might be needed with a view to establishing standards for the performance of the work and related training opportunities, especially for young people. It may, for example, be in the public interest to devise standards of work and training under the regulation of professional bodies for employment on new products or processes that affect the health and safety of consumers.

56. Encouragement to continue into and complete upper secondary education. Most Member countries seek to encourage the voluntary extension of education in order to improve individual chances and also raise the competences of the labour force. For this purpose more than exhortation is needed. The choice of whether to continue into upper secondary education, and of what kind, or whether to get a job is a complex one that is best made on the basis of the interests and abilities of the individual and the range of opportunities available, together with advice about the consequences of the alternatives. An effective policy of encouraging pupils to continue their education may entail a series of efforts by education and manpower authorities. For example, in Sweden the authorities concerned have developed a sequence of actions by which they observe during several months the movements of students leaving grade 9 and provide both educational and employment counselling and placement services accordingly. In 1976 Canada introduced a job exploration programme by which potential "drop-out" students can obtain up to nine weeks' work in order to help them assess more realistically some of the consequences of leaving school.

57. In view of the fact that many students "drop-out" of secondary school, as a way of encouraging them to complete this part of their education it seems worth considering improving its content in relation to working life and to changes in individual aspirations and attitudes about which relatively little specific information is yet available. Empirical research in these matters is urgently needed. Since it is

* See Review of National Policies for Education: Netherlands, OECD, Paris, 1976

often their social background that leads many students to try to enter the labour force from compulsory school while others benefit from continued education, it seems desirable that society should give assistance or support, including initial training and employment opportunities, to all young people who enter the labour force before the age of 18. This support should be given according to individual need and be comparable with that given to those who stay on at school.

58. Financial support. A complementary measure is to ensure that students do not fail to enter or complete upper secondary education for lack of financial resources. Recognising that the socio-economic status of the families of many young people can confer significantly unequal chances, many countries already provide a limited amount of financial aid through tax allowances to parents, family allowances and grants. The extension of financial aid to permit education up to the minimum working age (as in Spain) or the completion of upper secondary education appears to be an important condition of creating more equal opportunities, and merits detailed consideration by governments. While some countries do not provide such aid selectivity, others may do so especially under conditions of financial stringency.

2. Preparation for working life during upper secondary education

59. In most Member countries the majority of young people enter the labour force between the ages of 16 and 19, whether they "drop-out" of upper secondary school or complete it. Yet upper secondary education is still to a large extent conceived as preparation for transfer to higher education, whether academic or higher technical, rather than as preparation for working life. This problem has been aggravated by the massive increase during recent years of enrolments in upper secondary education, partly as a result of changes in demographic structure but mainly because of increased transfer rates from compulsory education which have brought to this level a much more diversified student population. There is, therefore, an urgent need to make upper secondary education more directly relevant to entry to working life. For this purpose major changes are needed. The following main approaches can be considered.

i) New relationships between general and vocational education

60. In non-European Member countries it is possible for most students to study both general and vocational subjects in the upper secondary school. In most European countries there are separate streams or institutions oriented towards either higher education or employment. There are pedagogical reasons for thinking that the division of abilities into the traditional categories of academic, intellectual or theoretical in one hand and practical, manual or technical on the other is false:

34

manual or technical training can have a general educational value, and general education can be relevant to employment. The difference in status between general and vocational education contributes to generating and perpetuating social disparities and also leads to less than satisfactory utilisation of human abilities and to dissatisfaction in employment. The organisation of education at this level should be reformed to permit a greater diversification of studies with a view to enabling apparently general and vocational subjects to be studied at the same time.

61. The feasibility of such an approach is well illustrated by the inclusion of languages or mathematics in vocational training and of technical subjects in general education. The simultaneous pursuit of general education objectives and preparation for working life implies the need to bring different types of institutions into a more coherent framework. It also implies a need to reorganise curricula with a view to promoting flexible movements among studies, which can allow errors of choice to be corrected. There is a need to devise a variety of new approaches in an experimental spirit. A promising innovation appears to be the creation of arrangements which enable students to combine formal education, general preparation for working life, some specific vocational preparation and some initial work experience. While in some cases they may be a useful preliminary to commitment to a particular occupation, it is desirable that they should primarily help extend the ranges of students' knowledge and choice about working life.

62. The possibilities of innovation are illustrated by the French law of 11th July of 1975, which among other things aims to give technical colleges the status of lycées and to introduce manual, technical and technological subjects into the curriculum; or by projects in some German Laender to offer in the upper grades of the Gymnasium (the traditional general preparation for university) combinations of courses that lead to full vocational qualification in such fields as technology or clerical work.

ii) Certificates in upper secondary education

63. In many countries students who complete the academic streams of upper secondary school leave with a diploma that certifies completion of a cycle of studies and has limited practical use in employment. Most students are assessed according to relative ability or performance in order to select those who are thought most suitable for higher education. The effect of this hierarchical assessment is that the remainder, together with those who do not complete upper secondary education, are regarded by many employers as second-rate or even as failures, even though they may have obtained vocational diplomas. Yet together they are the largest group of new entrants to the labour force. There is thus an urgent need to review certification practices so that the

qualifications of those who leave at any time during upper secondary education, or at the end of each of its main streams, are relevant to entry into employment and comparable with the qualifications of those who continue their education. To this end, it would be preferable for certificates to describe the content of the subjects studied with a view to helping indicate the competences of the individual. Employers and workers' representatives could play a significant role in the design of curricula, courses of study and of certificates, and in securing their recognition. The status of vocational training with general education could be raised if educational credit were given for training, including some training by enterprises, especially in criteria for admission to higher technical and scientific education.

iii) Work experience during upper secondary education

64. Although it is widely recognised that learning by experience is an important complement to conceptual learning, the opportunities for acquiring work experience while still at school remain limited. The more extensive opportunities in countries such as Canada, New Zealand and the United States for school students to work during holidays or part-time in the evenings and weekends enables many of them to finance further studies as well as learning about work; but they raise complex problems of whether students should be considered as part of the labour force and be covered by unemployment compensation programmes. Formal arrangements to link education courses with periods of related practical work tend to be limited to apprenticeship in traditional trades and in higher education to certain disciplines such as health professions, engineering and architecture, some welfare education (e.g. for probation work) and language training. These schemes tend not to be applied uniformly and vary in design and effectiveness or according to whether or not they are required by law.

65. The scope for providing work experience for upper secondary students is wider than for those in compulsory education, simply because they are older, further advanced in adolescence, have had relatively longer to become consciously interested in themselves and in abstract ideas and learning, are relatively better placed to consider the choice of an initial job or even of a career, and more likely to be of use to employers. Most Canadian provinces have arrangements for work experience. For example, a number of Saskatchewan high schools are engaging in programmes to give work experience to students in commercial and technical studies for varying periods on full-day, part-day or staggered-day schedules.

66. It seems desirable for governments to promote collaboration among schools and employers with a view to developing opportunities for work experience for the majority of students who are likely to go straight into the labour force. There may be a special role for local

authorities and voluntary bodies to create work opportunities for students in their localities. In doing so, it is important to ensure that students can do work related to the needs of employers as well as to their own needs and that the school helps students prepare for such periods of work and engage in an appropriate follow-up activity when back in school. In view of the obvious dangers of failing on the one hand to provide significant experience to students and on the other of interrupting production, it would be desirable for the education and manpower authorities to make a special examination of the feasibility and regulation of work experience. The questions of whether and at what rate students should be paid, of their liability for social security contributions, their protection against industrial injuries, etc. and of the capital and current costs to employers require careful consideration.

3. Entry to employment from upper secondary education

i) Normal entry

67. Many of the difficulties experienced by young people in the transition to working life would be reduced if the changes suggested above were implemented. There is a need to recognise the principle that education at the upper secondary level should include sufficient vocational content to qualify all students to obtain a first job and also to enable them to continue to learn through formal instruction or from their own work experience. It is in the public interest for governments to provide basic training for those who for a variety of reasons did not attain a sufficient level at school. It is in employers' interest to provide more complete and effective induction training.

ii) Special job creation

68. Many of those who have already left upper secondary school have difficulty in finding employment under present employment conditions, especially those who have pursued more general studies. In addition to the possibilities of employment creation in the private and public sectors already discussed, recent experience has demonstrated the feasibility of governments acting directly to finance non-profit-making community projects that also create employment. While they are not confined to young people such projects can, in times of continuing high unemployment, help them engage in constructive activities which satisfy the strong sense of social responsibility that many of them have and help reduce the depressive effect of being out of work. These initiatives have generally been welcomed, and have had favourable effects in helping young people acquire work experience. While few have been formally evaluated, it has been estimated by the Canadian

authorities that the Local Initiatives Programme has significantly increased the GNP, as well as creating jobs more quickly than by traditional public works measures. This type of approach may be most relevant in countries that do not yet have a long tradition of voluntary social work. Where it is used it can be designed to incorporate training.

iii) The risk of unemployment

69. In spite of efforts to reduce employment, levels of manpower utilisation are expected to remain relatively low during the next few years. There is a special need for realistic counselling about employment possibilities and the alternatives available to young people, such as community service and training, and for governments providing special training.

70. Measures which promote employment or increase future employability through extended education and training can represent a more positive use of financial resources than the payment of unemployment benefits with the psychological effects that they have on the individual, and can also be less inflationary. Moreover, the fact that public expenditures on them can be offset by savings on payments to the unemployed and by the tax revenues from their employment makes it possible to apply them on a larger scale than if governments had to bear the full outlay.

D. HIGHER EDUCATION

1. The long-term trend in the demand for higher education

71. The very strong individual demand for higher education, which is now spreading among adults, continues in large measure to be governed by the social and economic status that it has acquired. The sum total of these demands is still rising. Although its composition changes in relation to students' perceptions of career prospects in different occupations, the total demand for higher education appears to be autonomous and not conditioned by specific employment prospects. It shows little sign of being contained by or adapting itself to the currently and prospectively limited and uncertain overall employment prospects for graduates, especially in the public sector, including teaching, which until recently has absorbed a very high proportion of them. A central problem is to what extent and by what means this demand can be satisfied : on one hand it is recognised that higher education has a vital contribution to make to economic development and employment and that its cultural objectives are specially important:

yet on the other hand it has to be borne in mind that there are limitations on resources, that other levels of education have competing claims, and that many countries are concerned to provide a more equitable access to education within society.

2. Higher technical and professional education

72. One approach to meeting these sometimes conflicting objectives has been through the diversification of higher education, particularly by the creation of new institutions of higher technical and vocational education (whether short or long-cycle), partly as a deliberate policy by governments to provide lower-cost alternatives to traditional universities.

73. The expansion of short-cycle institutions has been a marked feature of policy in North America and has more recently spread in Europe. In Germany the short-cycle institutes created in 1969 offer a full alternative route to higher education through vocational training.

74. Many of them have been successful in terms of status, quality of instruction and of the employability of their graduates.* For example, the Community Colleges in Canada are providing opportunities, both for young people and for older workers returning from the labour force, to complement their secondary education with a wide range of vocational and technical courses. The approach of combining training in these Colleges with training in enterprises has been welcomed by students and employers alike, and ways are being sought to strengthen their inter-connections still further in order to make the best use of both. As a matter a policy students can receive training allowances or other forms of financial help according to individual need.

75. Since graduates from short-cycle professional and technical education tend to be absorbed into employment relatively more easily than people without specific qualifications, a shift in the balance of enrolments in favour of short-cycle and more professional and technical education can help ease the problem of finding employment for those who take general studies. Such a change of emphasis is easier to achieve with growing populations and increasing resources, but may be more imperative for countries where these features do not apply.

76. It has been suggested that the balance of resources can also be shifted in favour of more professional and technical education by reducing the length of studies at the beginning of general higher education. Proposals to do so have been made in Germany and the Netherlands.

77. The more the institutional capacity for specific technical and professional education expands, especially to levels approved by

*
See Short-cycle Higher Education: A Search for Identify, OECD, 1973.

professional licensing bodies, the greater is the difficulty of all graduates from such institutions in finding employment in the specific field they have studied. Because of the high cost of such education it is essential to plan capacity. There is however a danger that, when doing so, education and manpower authorities will allow themselves to be too closely guided by the unimaginative types of projections of future occupational patterns of employment, which have been shown by experience to ignore mobility in employment. The inter-occupational mobility that takes place is in fact highly desirable for its own sake and cannot be taken to indicate bad planning or poor choice. In large-part, it reflects the fact that many work functions are common to several apparently different jobs or occupations. It is desirable that students should be able to alter their choices in the light of their education, and that enrolments in different branches of study should not fluctuate so widely as to create costly and frustrating changes of career plans.

78.   More open access to higher technical and professional education to graduates from lower levels of vocational training can also help to reduce social disparities.

   3.   General Higher Education

79.   There is a growing problem of employment for those who pursue general arts, liberal studies, and the social sciences. Some students who choose these disciplines may do so for their intrinsic interest, and so express a "social" rather than an "economic" demand for education, while others may not have developed firm career aspirations. By definition, it is impossible for them all to be employed in these fields; yet in practice, many students acquire aspirations to remain in them.

80.   This problem has given rise to political difficulties in some countries. On the one hand, students in higher education have come to protest vigorously either at the lack of sufficient or related employment opportunities or at suggestions to reduce places in education. On the other hand, many members of the public who bear the fiscal burden of education, including the high cost of university education, are showing signs of resisting the growth of public expenditures in this sector. Not all those who have already benefited from heavy expenditure on their education can expect to have jobs created which directly utilise their current knowledge and ability, especially in subjects such as the liberal arts and humanities, but they can reasonably be expected to take part in the productive activity of society and to acquire the necessary skills. There is a role for more realistic counselling before entry to higher education as well as on entry into the labour force.

81.   The solution partly depends upon society deciding how it wishes
to allocate its resources among the various sectors of education and
age groups.   There are competing claims on grounds of equity to
expand the educational facilities and opportunities for upper secondary
education, to provide remedial education for those who are slow to
learn and to expand adult education.   While there is a need on grounds
of efficiency to provide the scientific and technical knowledge needed
for the development, management, operation and control of modern
technological systems, and ultimately to create the growth of resources
for more general cultural purposes, there is a complementary need
to discriminate in their utilisation in the long-term process of social
development.   There is thus a case for combining general education
with other technical education in much the same way as has been
suggested during upper secondary education.   This, combined with
arrangements to permit upward mobility from vocational training, could
help widen social opportunities considerably.

4.   Work experience for students in higher education

82.   Opportunities for students in higher education to obtain clinical
or practical experience of their field of study are well known.   In
Italy many students do part-time work.   In Sweden employers in the
private sector frequently prefer to hire graduates who have previously
had lower level jobs.

E.   COMPETENCES USED IN EMPLOYMENT

83.   At all levels of education and training, curricula could be designed
in closer relation to employment without losing sight of the other purposes of education.   The work functions performed by individuals, the
organisation of work within enterprises, management, decision-making,
negotiation and consultation (all of which are continuously modified by
changes in the economy, markets, production methods, technology
and scales of production) call for a range of personal and technical
qualities in the labour force which form part of the total and much
wider set of competences needed in adult life in modern society.   For
example, it is clear that several different types of competences are
used in working life in various combinations according to the job
performed.   They include such categories as:

   i)   the ability to read, calculate and comprehend, and to
        communicate orally and in writing;
   ii) the basic technical knowledge, skills and understanding
        used at various levels in a range of different jobs;

iii) the personal qualities that may be used in employment, such as the ability to participate in group action, to deal with the public, or to assume responsibility;

iv) the management of other abilities, such as mobilising information, making decisions and exercising judgement;

v) the ability to continue learning; and

vi) competences related to working life generally, such as knowing how to search for a job, the purposes and means of action by workers' associations, matters relating to the contract of employment such as pay, leave, rights, and duties in employment.

84. If education and training are to create opportunities for the acquisition of these competences at the required levels, an essential precondition of satisfactory curriculum development is to identify, through empirical surveys, the ones that are used, and for the authorities concerned to consult with representatives of workers and employers about the ones that need to be developed. A start could most usefully be made to consider the essential competencies that pupils should acquire during compulsory education. The criitical importance of curricula has been underlined by the British Government's decision to set up a Further Education Curriculum Review and Development Unit.

IV

MEASURES TO IMPROVE THE UTILISATION
OF THE EDUCATION AND TRAINING
OF THE LABOUR FORCE

85. The 1964 Recommendation on an Active Manpower Policy and the
1976 Recommendation on a General Employment and Manpower Policy
suggest the extended use of selective employment and manpower measures
to raise the level of employment, to stabilise it and to improve the utilisation of manpower. The utilisation of the education of the labour force
is a dimension that could receive more attention in the design and use of
these policies.

86. In a wider perspective the long-term prospects for the character
of economic growth cannot be ignored. Because, in some countries,
material economic growth of the kind enjoyed during most of the postwar years is unlikely to be sustained there appears to be a need to find
new ways of organising work in relation to education. Education can
make significant contributions to new approaches to social and economic
development if the education of the labour force is better utilised.

A. MEASURES TO IMPROVE THE UTILISATION
OF MANPOWER

87. The measures being devised to create employment opportunities
and to improve the quality of working life could more effectively promote
efficiency and individual work satisfaction if the structures of employment and the content of jobs were designed with the criterion of making
the fullest use of the educational levels of the labour force in mind. The
fact that levels of education will continue to rise in Member countries
creates a change in the quality of the labour force over and above its
mere numerical increase to which the content as well as the number
of jobs needs to be adapted.

1. Information about the education and training of the labour
force

88. While some data about the labour force by level of education are
available in many countries, there is a marked lack of information

43

about the labour force according to the training it has received. In most countries there is a major gap in information about training in enterprises or sponsored by employers compared with training in public institutitons or sponsored by governments. The availability and quality of this type of information varies greatly among countries and several improvements could be made fairly quickly. The experience of those countries (such as Canada) that have conducted special surveys may be helpful to other Member countries. Education and training authorities could provide better information to employers about the kinds of skills and abilities they can expect among graduates from each of the various levels and types of education and training.

2. Certification and credentials in employment

89. Education and certificates have for long been used by employers as selection criteria, sometimes in combination with work history, but often on their own, either as direct evidence of specific professional knowledge or as proxies for such qualities as intelligence, diligence, ability to reason or to go on learning; and they have been used by individuals in competing for jobs, especially the more desirable or well-paid ones. The rapid expansion of education in recent years has markedly increased competition for jobs according to the level of formal credentials. The higher proportion of young graduates than older, less highly educated people in many occupations may partly reflect a modification of job content in ways that utilise their different abilities, but it is highly probable that it also reflects a depreciation of formal qualifications. This form of selection operates in ways that may be both inequitable and inefficient by excluding many people who have the ability to perform a job, possibly even better than someone with higher formal credentials.

90. In the short term, governments can help private employers by providing technical advice and incentives. Several governments have modified their own selection processes so as to incorporate, in addition to formal credentials, knowledge and experience and personal qualities as far as they can be judged. Many employers, however, use educational credentials as a preliminary, apparently inexpensive selection device, but one which entails subsequently higher costs if they make a poor choice. The practice of specifying the possession of a given level of educational attainment can be as discriminatory as specifying sex or race if it is not relevant to a job. More positive alternatives have, however, yet to be evolved.

3. The development and utilisation of manpower by enterprises

91. Governments can also help promote the creation of jobs and improve the quality of working life by measures designed to help enterprises develop their own personnel policies and to promote the mutual
adaptation of their employment structures and the changing education
of the labour force. An OECD Study of Enterprise Manpower Management suggested that, in many enterprises, decisions about recruitment,
training, utilisation and lay-off are commonly subordinate to decisions
about production and fixed investment. It concluded that many enterprises could develop more positive manpower policies that form part
of, and are on a level with their overall corporate policies. In particular, employers could know much more about the education and
training characteristics of their own personnel. They could also be
helped to make use of information about the education and training of
the manpower available outside the enterprise, where there are often
scarcities of the types of manpower that are currently needed, or
surpluses that could be used after training.

92. Employment patterns have yet fully to reflect the expansion of
education, partly because unsuitable personnel planning techniques
often fail to take into account the changes in the labour force. The
changes in the levels of educational attainment arising from changes
in the pattern of enrolments among the various sectors of education
and from policies to shift the balance in favour of upper secondary and
short-cycle education will call for more positive adjustments in employment patterns and in recruiting policies. While some forward-
looking enterprises recognise that their competitivity and potential
expansion depends on the full utilisation of their personnel, it is
desirable that governments should find ways to help other employers
devise internal policies to take advantage of the continuous changes in
the composition of the labour force according to its levels of education.

93. Employers can also be encouraged to adapt their recruiting
policies in the short run and even to absorb a certain proportion of
the trained unemployed. In Canada special intensive recruitment
campaigns were undertaken in 1975 by the Canada Manpower Service in
collaboration with employers to encourage them to fill recorded and
unrecorded vacancies, to trace unemployed workers with relevant
skills and to ensure that appropriate assistance, such as mobility
grants, was available.

4. The creation of new jobs

94. Economic expansion and development depend significantly on the
growth in the number of jobs. Measures for the creation of permanent
jobs can be more forceful if they are designed to utilise the education

and training of the labour force and if they further extend it through specific forms of training. In addition to the expansion of existing enterprises the creation of new ones can be important in utilising rising education levels. The vi bility of new enterprises may to an increasing extent be governed by their effectiveness in mobilising human ability and potential. Efforts to increase employment at given levels of aggregate demand imply a need for new relationships between fixed capital, technology and manpower.

95. It should be remembered that employment includes the application of managerial skills which can have a vital impact on the patterns and content of employment. The establishment of new enterprises also depends heavily, and probably critically upon arrangements for the initial training of the personnel and all levels of management and more attention could be given to the potential of training for this purpose.

96. Action is also being taken to induce employers who are establishing new capital projects in selected regions to plan more explicitly the jobs that will be created. Moreover, if policies to develop specific regions are to be effective it may be specially important to try to check the loss of investment in education and training which occurs through migration to other parts of a country. Public expenditures on subsidies of this kind can be wholly or partly self-financing by the increase in taxes paid by new employees and savings in social security payments to them, depending on how rates of tax, payments and subsidies are set. This approach provides a special opportunity under current conditions to encourage employers to design jobs in relation to the levels of education and training of the labour force in their locality, including those with low level skills as well as higher levels of education.

97. In some countries governments are helping enterprises adapt their investment and production to evolving patterns of final demand. An example is the approach used in the Netherlands to help enterprises in difficulty to become viable by assisting them, if necessary, to change management, to develop different lines of production, replace capital equipment and obtain suitable personnel. This too offers scope to utilise the skills of the labour force. For this approach to be fully effective, complementary action is needed to provide specific training for the personnel and for management as well.

B. THE QUALITY OF WORKING LIFE

98. The trend towards devising policies for improving the quality of working life can be reinforced by education and training policies. The changing expectations formed during education and by the media and the

aspirations of many adults for opportunities for education and training, call for responses by employers to improve individual jobs and the organisation of work within enterprises, which, if they are to be realistic, depend partly on a greater awareness by employers of how attitudes are changing and of how other employers are meeting them, and partly on training management to become more concerned with these questions.

99.   Direct action to improve the quality of working life through measures to improve jobs is illustrated by the Swedish measure: enterprises are required, in times of high conjunctural activity, to set aside part of their profits which are released in times of recession for investment to improve the working environment.

100.   Action can also be taken to promote the kinds of investment that facilitate both a higher level of employment and a better utilisation of individual education and skills through assessments of the prospective consequences of capital projects.   Such action can be required under legislation or be induced by other means such as financing the assessments, providing information or technical advice.   An OECD study which examined the relationship between the manpower policies of governments and of enterprises suggested that it could be a prior condition of public authorisation of the finance or the location of an enterprise that an assessment should be made of the potential impacts on manpower in the enterprise and outside it.

101.   Realistic attempts to improve the quality of working life have to reconcile individual aspirations with what is economically feasible for the enterprise and for the economy.   The questions which concern workers can most clearly be identified at the level of the enterprise and solutions worked out by them in the framework of its decisions. Action by governments to help improve the quality of working life includes in some countries measures to promote new forms of consultation and decision-making in enterprises and participation by workers. A variety of innovations is being developed.   Their common element is to improve the ability of workers themselves to decide what changes in employment and training they wish to secure within their enterprises. The promotion of industrial democracy becomes an instrument of policy as well as an objective in itself.   In Germany, legislation requires Works' Councils to include workers' representatives and to develop manpower policies for the enterprise, but leaves them free to decide what aspects will be considered.   An example of what can be done beyond technical instruction for preparing workers to make the most of their life at work is provided by Norway, where there is a long tradition of workers' education, and the learning process has been seen as fundamental to the innovations in work organisation in recent years.   Both unions and employers have introduced special training arrangements to prepare representatives to serve on the new Corporate

Assemblies (a kind of supervisory board). Particularly interesting is the Training and Development Fund set up jointly by the Norwegian Employers and Trade Unions, which provides for weekly contributions from employers (1 kroner per worker) and workers (1/2 kroner), with a view to spreading information about education throughout Norwegian working life.

C. NEW LIFETIME PATTERNS OF EDUCATION, TRAINING AND WORK

102. There are reasons for thinking that the traditional sequence of education, working life and retirement, which is still the predominant pattern of life for most members of the labour force, may need to be modified. Within certain limits, to be educated in youth and to work when older is an obvious necessity, yet is not entirely natural: many people are more motivated to action than to learning in youth, and to reflection rather than action when older.

103. The need for opportunities for recurrent education has been recognized by some OECD countries. * Wider education and training opportunities for adults can help correct disparities introduced by unequal opportunities and social selection, especially during secondary education, help equalize educational attainment among age groups, aid the development of productivity during working life, and satisfy the aspirations of many adults for learning. The existence of an extensive system of adult education and training is an essential pre-condition of new lifetime patterns of work and study.

104. There is a corresponding need for flexibility in working life to help individuals exercise greater freedom of choice among work, learning and leisure.

105. Continuing and often unexpected changes in science and technology, the development of new knowledge, and changes in the structure and functioning of enterprises and economic systems make it imperative for members of the labour force to have further education and training opportunities which cannot always be provided by enterprises.

106. To promote a more equitable distribution of education and to permit members of the labour force to return to study, it would be possible to consider a basic right to a certain number of years of education for everyone financed by the state and irrespective of when it is exercised. For those who return to education during working life it

* See the Recommendation of the European Ministers of Education, Stockholm, 1975, based on the OECD Report on Recurrent Education.

may be necessary to consider either paid leave of absence or the payment of personal allowances which could be varied according to the
employment situation. Priority in admissions might be given according to one or more criteria such as lack of formal education, being
unemployed, or age. The right to educational leave, is a complementary one that could become more widespread. It could help promote a
more constructive use of periods of enforced idleness during working
life.

D. INEQUALITY AND POVERTY

107. Inequalities in education, employment, income, social status
and mobility are interconnected. Some people, often from favoured
socio-economic backgrounds, who choose academic or general courses
and perform well at each level, have access to privileged positions in
employment which are secure, interesting and well-paid. Conversely,
limited education and training, poor performance in school, lack of
work or of access to employment at socially acceptable rates of pay
with opportunities for development are some of the basic causes of
inequalities and poverty. Other sources lie in the structures of employment such as endogenous trends in technology, accelerated by public
expenditures and fixed investment subsidies, which promote a widening
range of jobs according to skill level; while international flows of
migrant workers have helped maintain the least desirable kinds of work
which many domestic workers are unwilling to perform.

108. Action to achieve more equitable access to education and to
employment can make a significant contribution to reducing poverty and
improving productive efficiency, as well as being an objective of value
in itself as an important condition of social progress. It can also make
a contribution to policies for income redistribution and help ease some
of the burden placed on income transfers. There is a growing need to
satisfy the aspirations for more equitable opportunities for real satis-
factions throughout life that are generated in various ways, such as by
extended education, by the attention given to wage bargaining about
differentials, and by growing concern with extremes of life styles.

109. There is a need for an ensemble of measures in education and
employment policies to reduce inequalities and poverty. Action in
education alone may remain ineffective if it is not complemented by
measures to improve opportunities throughout working life, and the
effectiveness of manpower and employment measures to improve
opportunities depends on improving the education and training of the
least well-prepared members of the current or potential labour force.
A consistent policy approach could aim to extend the benefits of

education more fairly and reduce the costs of employment that fall most heavily on incumbents, especially the lack of opportunities for individuals to utilize their education in their employment.

110.   Extending the benefits of education more fairly entails several major changes in policy.   There is a need to provide better basic education for all children in order to improve lifetime learning capacity and access to higher levels of education.   There is a need to reduce the artificial distinction between general and vocational types of education by bringing them together in the curriculum and in institutions, devising more extensive possibilities for transfer among courses and more equal opportunities for students in different streams to obtain access to the next level of education which will not be limited by lack of financial means.   It is desirable that the terms of student finance should enable young people between 16 and 19 to pursue their education without undue sacrifices by other members of the family.   Measures are needed to enable students who enter the labour force without completing upper secondary education to obtain a broadly equivalent level of training in public institutions or enterprises until the age of 18. Providing more equitable training opportunities throughout working life would entail redeploying resources to help provide it for those whose training costs are higher than average.   More opportunities for adult education can help adjust differences of attainment among age groups.

111.   Reducing disparities in employment depends on the vigorous application of the Recommendation on a General Employment and Manpower Policy adopted by the Council of the OECD in March 1976 which gives a prominent place to "promoting more equity in the distribution of employment opportunities".   The Recommendation envisages a range of actions designed to create more employment at given levels of aggregate demand pressure which can significantly improve the situation of many people whose employability is low.

112.   In this connection there is a special concern for the large numbers of young people who are unsuited for employment when they leave school. The reasons for their unsuitability are not as well known as they should be; but it is clear that they include low levels of education and lack of specific skills related to poor performance or early leaving or the lack of vocational preparation in many schools; ignorance of training and employment opportunities; poor motivation and ignorance by these young people of their own potential interests and abilities; the preferences of many employers for young people with formal credentials and some experience, or for older workers. When such young people can obtain work it is likely to be unskilled, often unstable and poorly paid; and once employed in that category they find it difficult to move to more stable and satisfying work. The primary objective of policy strategies to deal with the employment of these young people

should be to ensure that they do not remain in low level types of employment, but are helped to enter more normal kinds of jobs. With this in mind some countries are finding that only a combination of several types of action is effective. In the long run there is a need to bring together the measures discussed in Part IV of this report, especially during compulsory and secondary education. In the short term, action can focus on those who have already entered the labour force. For them the experimental projects being developed to create first jobs combined with personal advice and some initial training are promising. The participation in these projects of experienced workers and non-governmental institutions indicates widespread concern within the community, willingness to assume responsibility towards young people in difficulty and may be a vital element in their success. The question that arises is to what extent action of this type can be replicated to a sufficient extent to deal with the magnitude of the problem.

113. Measures can also include action to modify investment incentives to act on employment as well, to reduce barriers to access to employment, to enrich job content in many cases, to open training to many who do not at present receive it, and to raise the status of manual work.

114. Such improvements entail costs to the community. A question however arises about the extent to which enterprises are able directly to bear these costs. Some enterprises are able to bear them in the first instance; but many others are obliged to follow a commercial rationality which does not permit them to pursue the human and social objectives of improving employment opportunities and conditions as fully as many of them wish. In some cases, the additional internal costs to enterprises can be externalised by the use of selected financial assistance and incentives. Such measures can represent a better deployment of public resources than outlays on remedying some of the consequences of unequal employment (e. g. outlays on unemployment benefit, on public pensions or on remedial health care on disabilities incurred during employment). The costs to the community may have to be absorbed slowly by establishing priorities in favour of those who are worst off. For example, in France measures to upgrade the status of manual work provide earlier retirement selectively for those who have worked for a significant time on dirty, noisy or repetitive work.

V

POLICY INSTRUMENTS

A. THE CO-ORDINATION OF POLICIES FOR EDUCATION AND WORKING LIFE

115.   It is feasible to bring the policies in education and working life into closer relationship with each other because they are both concerned with dynamic systems in a state of continuous transformation and interaction; each capable in different ways of responding to changes in public aspirations and expectations.   However, these systems have quite different structures, function differently, and are affected by policies formulated through different processes.   Education is predominantly a public service, created and made available through large administrative systems in which policy is implemented by the public authorities in the light of broad political judgements and decisions reflecting the needs and wishes of the community and the electorate.   In contrast, working life has its place within economies that combine in varying degrees the management and free operation of the market for goods and services, in which employment is heavily dependent on production and investment, and on decisions by enterprises and workers' organisations that may be outside the scope of public policy.   An awareness of the extent to which education and working life operate within different systems therefore becomes particularly important when considering co-ordination not only among government departments and among the various levels of government, but also between the policies of governments and those of enterprises and workers' representatives.

116.   Significant policy progress could be made simply by initiating arrangements for collaboration within countries, bearing in mind that it is not necessarily assured by creating institutions.   There is a special need to create conditions in which action can originate at the local level where problems can often best be recognized and acceptable solutions worked out.   Since the action of many branches of government has an influence on education and employment, an impulse to progress in bringing them into closer and more effective relationships can be given if the highest levels of government call upon all ministries and levels of government to take their objectives for education and working life into full consideration in the application and management of all their policies, services and programmes.

B. THE ORGANISATION OF CURRICULA

117.   The guiding principle on which curricula might most usefully
be organised among the levels of education and training is to make it
as polyvalent as possible with respect to the range of options at the
end of each level (i. e. either transfer to the next level or to employment) with a view to enabling the choice of education and training
courses and careers to be made as late as may be consistent with the
need for specific preparation in some types of employment.

118.   There is scope for the more widespread use of curricula based
on sets of modules that can be cumulated into various coherent groups
offering considerable potential for relating education and training to
individual interests and learning speeds as well as to various groups
of employment possibilities and changes in them.   It has been suggested
that they can help individuals assess their own progress and be
examined with less risk of complete failure, and contribute to flexible
movements within education and training.   After the initial investment
in development, such curricula are less costly in terms of expenditure,
learning time, individual effort and reduced risk of failure.   The
extended use of modular curricula raises pedagogical questions and
problems of co-ordination among institutions that need to be examined.

119.   In this way much of the fragmentation of education and training
among different levels and types of institutions, including enterprises,
could be reduced, while their autonomy could be maintained. There is
a special need for more extensive opportunities for upward movement
in training and employment from the manual to the technical, technological, higher professional and scientific levels and for interchanges
with general education which are comparable with the possibilities for
upward academic mobility.

120.   In view of the many "blind alley" jobs that still exist there is
scope in most countries for individuals qualified in a trade or technical
function to obtain higher employment qualifications by adding supplementary courses and thus minimising opportunity costs and expenditures.
France and Sweden have introduced measures to this end.

C. TECHNICAL AND VOCATIONAL EDUCATION
AND TRAINING

121.   Technical and vocational education and training is one of the
more important policy instruments that brings the worlds of education
and work closer together.   They are forms of instruction which
provide major means of raising the productive capacity and efficiency

of the economy and of enterprises, improving individual well-being
and of helping correct social disparities in employment. Their full and
effective use raises many issues which yet need to be clearly identified
and examined. *

122.   Responsibilities for the provision of training services and their
financing are shared in many different ways within each Member country among different levels of government, the public sector (in schools,
various institutions of higher education, public training institutions
and within the public authorities) and the private sector (in enterprises
and private schools of business, etc.). Recognizing that these patterns
of responsibilities reflect different interests, and in some countries
different constitutional arrangements, but that they are interrelated
in highly complex ways, there is a need to agree common objectives
and means of collaboration. The United Kingdom has already taken
certain steps to this end, most notably through the pilot schemes of
unified vocational preparation referred to in paragraph 50 above. These
are a joint venture by the United Kingdom education departments and
the Training Services Agency. In another, more recent development,
the Manpower Services Commission and the Department of Education
and Science have jointly set up a Training and Further Education
Consultative Group to provide a national forum for discussing matters
of common interest to the training and education services in England
and Wales.

123.   The role of government is to ensure that adequate opportunities
are available for all new entrants to the labour force to acquire a basic
occupational training and for adults to obtain further training, and
that enterprises are not compelled to reduce current or potential production for lack of appropriately capable manpower. To some extent
governments have a choice between training the domestic labour force,
bringing in trained immigrants and modifying production. Enterprises
have a comparable choice between training their personnel, recruiting
ready-trained manpower and changing production methods. Current
and future limits on immigration, inflows of foreign workers and on
fixed investment will undoubtedly make training a more crucial part of
economic policy, and suggest the need for a full examination of how it
could be developed for that purpose.

124.   Special attention should be given to increasing training opportunities for new entrants to the labour force in view of the fact that in
many OECD countries a significant proportion leave school without
any such training. It is highly desirable to ensure that this training
includes practical experience as well as classroom instruction. This

---

*   The Joint Working Party welcomes the opportunity for these questions to be
more fully considered at the Intergovernmental Meeting on Vocational Education and Training scheduled in 1978 under the work programme of the Education Committee.

can be done through extensions of formal education that incorporate practical work while the individual preserves his status as a student, or through more employment opportunities which combine instruction for young workers. The scale of the problem present a difficult choice for some countries under current employment conditions, but experience suggests that measures to create employment with training are of particular relevance to many young people who leave school early with low levels of attainment. In this connection pre-apprenticeship can be valuable for some occupations. Opportunities for work experience during education can be considered for the longer term objective of easing the transition of working life, bearing in mind the time needed to design appropriate types of experience and to guide students through them.

125. It is now recognized by all OECD countries that training has an essential contra-cyclical role since it can, if mobilized quickly to deal with the skill shortages that occur even in recession, help raise employment and at the same time reduce cost-inflationary pressures. The urgent need to provide training for the unemployed and training related to current skill shortages should not divert attention from the longer-term objective of training the employed, especially in view of the special difficulties at present of identifying future needs and increasing investment in training.

126. Experience of the design and management of training services whether in public training institutions or enterprises suggests the need to devise means for relating training to employment, which are more satisfactory to individuals, to enterprises and to the economy.

127. i) Training in public institutions. One approach that is fairly widely used is to provide training in public institutions according to the number of individuals who seek training. This approach is somewhat passive. Individuals can recognize personal preferences more readily than future employment possibilities, and many are inhibited by the low social status of both training and manual work, and by unsuitable teaching methods. One possible solution to these difficulties lies in giving administrators in the public employment service a responsibility to recommend training to people seeking jobs and the authority to provide them with an appropriate course. It is, however, hard to judge whether this method, which is used, for example, in the Canada Manpower Service, is broadly successful in generating a sufficient volume of training or meeting specific needs. In Sweden, training is provided each year for more than 100,000 people who run the risk of being unemployed. It takes place in public training centres, in the regular school system and in enterprises. It is jointly planned and provided by the National Labour Market Board and the National Board of Education in collaboration with employers' associations and trade unions. The final decision about training and financial support is taken by the local

or regional labour market authorities, and applicants for training are informed by officers of the public employment service if they are accepted.

128. ii) Training by enterprises. An alternative is to induce more training by enterprises. They are able to identify their own needs, but may give more attention to meeting current scarcities than to creating capacity for future development. The problem is complicated because a large but unknown proportion of the training effort of some countries takes place informally within enterprises, and because a small proportion of enterprises provides most of the training. The financial mechanisms that have been devised have helped share the costs among enterprises but have yet to generate a sufficient total amount of investment for the economy as a whole. While governments can provide supplementary finance, this should not be seen as a substitute for regular financing by enterprises themselves.

129. For example, the Industrial Training Act, 1964, in the United Kingdom, and the Employment and Training Act, 1973, have helped induce employers to devise more positive policies to provide training in relation to their internal needs and to improve its quality, but have not generated sufficient financial resources from each industry branch for training in the transferable skills needed by the branch. For this reason the United Kingdom authorities are examining the feasibility of new financing arrangements.

130. iii) Modular training for work functions. A satisfactory alternative approach to forward-looking decision-making about training services has yet to be developed. In view of the high degree of mobility in employment, the desirability of facilitating the maximum degree of free choice by individuals in education and in employment, and the need of the economy to achieve a continuous redeployment of manpower, it may be that the development of a more practical approach to assessing how to relate training to future employment will depend on modifying existing concepts and descriptions of occupation as a basis for employment preparation by adapting them to cover related types of employment. The mobility among occupations is undoubtedly possible because many work functions in different occupations are similar.

131. For this reason it appears necessary and realistic to devise new concepts and descriptions of employment. Analyses in progress in some countries (France, Germany and the United Kingdom) suggest that it may be both desirable and feasible for education and training to be related to those work functions through more polyvalent organisation of curricula (see paragraphs 117 through 120 above). The modules can be combined by individuals according to their interests and abilities, and by employers in ways that help relate the organisation of work in the enterprise to the qualifications of the available manpower. Since the structures of employment and the content of jobs are in fact in a state of

continuous change and dynamic development, it is preferable for education and training to be designed with these realities in mind. Moreover, it is unrealistic to attempt to train for all aspects of an occupation. Public outlays and individual effort can be reduced if training is directed instead towards something more limited, such as work functions of jobs, and the dependence on narrow occupational forecasting can be avoided.

D. INFORMATION AND COUNSELLING

132.   Information and advice about education, training and employment is a process of special importance in helping individuals to develop their abilities and interests and apply them during working life. Both the education and the manpower authorities provide separate education and employment counselling services, yet according to considerations that are not always clear, and which often differ, or even conflict. There appears to be a need for information and advice by the different authorities that is coherent and consistent, based on clear guiding principles and, above all realistically related to individual abilities and desires, the general employment situation and specific employment possibilities in the short-term, and uncertainties about future employment prospects. In view of the obvious dangers of contradiction, it seems desirable for common services to be provided to the public, but not necessarily a single one.

133.   Education and training institutions and enterprises have a corresponding need for information on which to base their decisions about what opportunities to provide and what form they should take, i.e. what courses, for whom, and with what methods; and what jobs for whom, and with what content in what organisation of work. The most common approach of giving information and advice to individuals about employment (whether general about working life, or specific about employers, jobs, conditions) implies that individuals should adapt to jobs. In the short run, this may be realistic, but there is a danger that when jobs are relatively scarce, competition for available jobs will be based on formal credentials leaving those without them in a weak position.

134.   In view of the complexity of the question an examination is urgently needed of the basis upon which information and advice can be provided for education and working life. The objectives of policy have to be made more clear with respect to how individuals should be guided. If free choice is an important objective in itself there is a case for providing information rather than advice. There may be a special need for advice in educational counselling. If so, the basis on which it is

given and procedures for consultation with parents, would be the subject of special concern. Such a study should take account of the needs of individuals at different stages of life, the different personal and technical qualities used in employment, and the needs of educational institutions and employers to make decisions about the development of individuals and their potential contribution to productivity.

135. Counselling services are under strain to advise on employment prospects and are exposed to criticism when there are scarcities of jobs or of manpower. Yet for the reasons already mentioned, it is only realistic to suppose that there will not be a correspondence between the numbers of people qualified in each occupation and the numbers of jobs becoming vacant at the time such people enter the labour force. This underlines once more the need for curricula to be so designed that individual ability and performance may be kept under continuous review during education and training; and that a much greater degree of flexibility on entry into employment and during working life may be encouraged.

136. The more the quality and relevance of information and advice improves, the more important it is to ensure that such services are readily available. Technical innovation in computers has made it possible for detailed information to be accumulated, stored and distributed. There is now a range of experience in the management and dissemination of such information which suggests that the selection of relevant information is the critical consideration. The Career Information System in Oregon, USA, is a particularly interesting application because it illustrates how, despite the high costs of computer systems, notably the marginal costs of adding information, a system can become financially viable on the basis of a small fee paid by the school, at the rate of $2 to $3 per student. Governments can, as in the Oregon case, subsidize the initial development costs as a means of achieving a wide impact within their financial constraints. This approach is now being extended to other states. Other countries take the view that counselling should be free-of-charge to the individual.

E. DIAGNOSES AND ASSESSMENTS

137. Much fundamental research is needed into the nature and functioning of interactions between education and employment, but action to deal with the urgent problems in OECD countries cannot wait for the results of long-term studies. Short-term diagnoses of the main problems are urgently needed, together with early assessments of the results of the measures being taken.

138.   A high priority is to obtain more detailed quantitative and
qualitative knowledge and deeper insights into the flows of people
between education and employment in order that measures may be
more closely related to the different problems of various categories.
Data about them, which is currently too broad and general, could be
related to the flows from the main levels of education and training
(including primary, secondary, initial vocational, apprenticeship,
further training).   Some of these flows need to be better understood:
for example, the problems of those who leave early from upper
secondary school are different from those who complete it and obtain
an academic qualification, and vary greatly according to local
circumstances.   There is also a need to distinguish the problems of
students moving into each level and type of education, who are still
the concern of education authorities, from those who have already left
education, and whose employment concerns the manpower authorities.
In the latter case data is needed about whether they enter the labour
force or not, and about the nature of their employment experience.
Data about the duration of unemployment of new entrants compared
with other age groups is an important guide to a balanced consideration
of policy priorities.   In the search for concrete solutions, which often
can only be found through collaboration among various agencies and
institutions at the local level, the prime need is for data of a more
detailed nature than can be provided by general statistics about flows.
Efforts should be aimed at the systematic and concrete utilization of
the data that is acquired by local agencies in the course of managing
their operations.

139.   Much could be done to explain the great variation in the time
that it takes one individual as opposed to another to become satisfactorily
established in working life and the conditions under which this occurs,
and why for some people the process merges into continuing career
development, while others have continuing difficulties in finding and
maintaining satisfactory employment at socially acceptable rates of pay.
It is obvious that experience during the early years of working life
can significantly affect the ways in which attitudes and skills develop,
and so influence the rest of working life.   Yet relatively little is known
about this phase.   Much could be learned from practical programmes
to examine what happens during it.   For example, in France, the
Centre d'Etudes et de Recherches sur les Qualifications (CEREQ) has
recently been entrusted by the Ministries for Education, Industry and
Labour, the Commissariat du Plan, and l'Institut National de la Statis-
tique et des Etudes Economiques to establish an "Observatoire
national" of entries into working life.   It will examine the conditions of
the transition from the various levels and types of education to working life, notably among young people, and observe the initial stages of
careers according to the knowledge acquired and the needs for continuing
education.

140.   It is also obvious that the values, motivations, attitudes and expectations of young people concerning education, training, employment, careers, pay, working conditions, freedom of choice and expression are significantly different from those of older age groups in society.   Moreover, these attitudes vary widely, and differ according to social background.   It has been suggested that vocational motivation ranks very high in individuals' decisions about their educational choices. *   These values and attitudes are clearly affected by a wide range of influences including family, urban life, television and other media, and experience during education, training and entry into the labour force.   The relevance, direction and credibility of government policies towards education and working life would be improved if they were based upon reliable empirical research into the attitudes of young people towards education and work, and also of older age groups and employers towards young people.

141.   It is also important to observe how overall patterns of employment, the content of jobs, and the emergence of new jobs are being affected by the major economic changes in progress in OECD countries and by success in expanding the application of selective manpower policies to create additional employment opportunities with a view to knowing to what extent new opportunities are being devised to utilize the education and training of the labour force.   Closely related is the need for empirical information about the competences that are used in working life and mobility among different types of employment.

142.   Policy measures, especially the large number of new types of initiative that are now being tried in Member countries, need to be assessed with a view to making an initial judgment of the scale and direction of their impact and also to examining the policy strategies that are quickly emerging.   International exchanges of views can help make new approaches known and improve their design.   Policy design and modification cannot wait for technical evaluations taking years to complete, although they may have their place.   Special care in assessing the new experimental measures is needed bearing in mind that what may be successful on a small scale cannot necessarily be applied more widely.   The measures most urgently requiring attention are :

    i)   modular forms of curriculum organisation;
    ii) special measures to create employment combined with training in the private and public sectors;
   iii) special direct job creation measures for unemployed young people, especially from the point of view of their usefulness in creating new forms of training;
    iv) new initiatives in information and counselling;

---

  *   See Individual Demand for Education, OECD (to be published).

v) alternative means of inducing more investment in training; and

vi) initiatives to link training and income support.

143. It is also desirable that governments should be able to assess policies as well as measures, particularly the major changes they may wish to introduce to create greater equality of opportunity in education within upper secondary education or among age groups; to give all new entrants to the labour force training for an initial employment; or to promote collaboration among local institutions.

OECD SALES AGENTS
DÉPOSITAIRES DES PUBLICATIONS DE L'OCDE

ARGENTINA – ARGENTINE
Carlos Hirsch S.R.L., Florida 165,
BUENOS-AIRES. ☎33-1787-2391 Y 30-7122

AUSTRALIA – AUSTRALIE
International B.C.N. Library Suppliers Pty Ltd.,
161 Sturt St., South MELBOURNE, Vic. 3205. ☎699-6388
658 Pittwater Road, BROOKVALE NSW 2100. ☎ 938 2267

AUSTRIA – AUTRICHE
Gerold and Co., Graben 31, WIEN 1. ☎52.22.35

BELGIUM – BELGIQUE
Librairie des Sciences,
Coudenberg 76-78, B 1000 BRUXELLES 1. ☎512-05-60

BRAZIL – BRÉSIL
Mestre Jou S.A., Rua Guaipá 518,
Caixa Postal 24090, 05089 SAO PAULO 10. ☎261-1920
Rua Senador Dantas 19 s/205-6, RIO DE JANEIRO GB.
☎ 232-07. 32

CANADA
Renouf Publishing Company Limited,
2182 St. Catherine Street West,
MONTREAL, Quebec H3H 1M7 ☎(514) 937-3519

DENMARK – DANEMARK
Munksgaards Boghandel,
Nørregade 6, 1165 KØBENHAVN K. ☎(01) 12 69 70

FINLAND – FINLANDE
Akateeminen Kirjakauppa
Keskuskatu 1, 00100 HELSINKI 10. ☎625.901

FRANCE
Bureau des Publications de l'OCDE,
2 rue André-Pascal, 75775 PARIS CEDEX 16.
☎524.81.67
Principal correspondant :
13602 AIX-EN-PROVENCE : Librairie de l'Université.
☎26.18.08

GERMANY – ALLEMAGNE
Verlag Weltarchiv G.m.b.H.
D 2000 HAMBURG 36, Neuer Jungfernstieg 21.
☎ 040-35-62-500

GREECE – GRÈCE
Librairie Kauffmann, 28 rue du Stade,
ATHÈNES 132. ☎322.21.60

HONG-KONG
Government Information Services,
Sales and Publications Office, Beaconsfield House, 1st floor,
Queen's Road, Central. ☎H-233191

ICELAND – ISLANDE
Snaebjörn Jónsson and Co., h.f.,
Hafnarstraeti 4 and 9, P.O.B. 1131, REYKJAVIC.
☎13133/14281/11936

INDIA – INDE
Oxford Book and Stationery Co.:
NEW DELHI, Scindia House. ☎45896
CALCUTTA, 17 Park Street. ☎240832

IRELAND - IRLANDE
Eason and Son, 40 Lower O'Connell Street,
P.O.B. 42, DUBLIN 1. ☎74 39 35

ISRAËL
Emanuel Brown: 35 Allenby Road, TEL AVIV. ☎51049/54082
also at:
9. Shlomzion Hamalka Street, JERUSALEM. ☎234807
48 Nahlath Benjamin Street, TEL AVIV. ☎53276

ITALY – ITALIE
Libreria Commissionaria Sansoni:
Via Lamarmora 45, 50121 FIRENZE. ☎579751
Via Bartolini 29, 20155 MILANO. ☎365083
Sous-dépositaires :
Editrice e Libreria Herder.
Piazza Montecitorio 120, 00 186 ROMA. ☎674628
Libreria Hoepli, Via Hoepli 5, 20121 MILANO. ☎365446
Libreria Lattes, Via Garibaldi 3, 10122 TORINO. ☎519274
La diffusione delle edizioni OCDE è inoltre assicurata dalle migliori
librerie nelle città più importanti.

JAPAN – JAPON
OECD Publications Centre,
Akasaka Park Building, 2-3-4 Akasaka, Minato-ku,
TOKYO 107. ☎586-2016

KOREA - CORÉE
Pan Korea Book Corporation,
P.O.Box n°101 Kwangwhamun, SÉOUL. ☎72-7369

LEBANON – LIBAN
Documenta Scientifica/Redico,
Edison Building, Bliss Street, P.O.Box 5641, BEIRUT.
☎354429–344425

THE NETHERLANDS – PAYS-BAS
W.P. Van Stockum,
Buitenhof 36, DEN HAAG. ☎070-65.68.08

NEW ZEALAND - NOUVELLE-ZÉLANDE
The Publications Manager,
Government Printing Office,
WELLINGTON: Mulgrave Street (Private Bag),
World Trade Centre, Cubacade, Cuba Street,
Rutherford House, Lambton Quay, ☎737-320
AUCKLAND: Rutland Street (P.O.Box 5344), ☎32.919
CHRISTCHURCH: 130 Oxford Tce (Private Bag), ☎50.331
HAMILTON: Barton Street (P.O.Box 857), ☎80.103
DUNEDIN: T & G Building, Princes Street (P.O.Box 1104),
☎78.294

NORWAY – NORVÈGE
Johan Grundt Tanums Bokhandel,
Karl Johansgate 41/43, OSLO 1. ☎02-332980

PAKISTAN
Mirza Book Agency, 65 Shahrah Quaid-E-Azam, LAHORE 3.
☎66839

PHILIPPINES
R.M. Garcia Publishing House, 903 Quezon Blvd. Ext.,
QUEZON CITY, P.O.Box 1860 – MANILA. ☎99.98.47

PORTUGAL
Livraria Portugal, Rua do Carmo 70-74, LISBOA 2. ☎360582/3

SPAIN – ESPAGNE
Mundi-Prensa Libros, S.A.
Castelló 37, Apartado 1223, MADRID-1. ☎275.46.55
Libreria Bastinos, Pelayo, 52, BARCELONA 1. ☎222.06.00

SWEDEN – SUÈDE
AB CE FRITZES KUNGL HOVBOKHANDEL,
Box 16 356, S 103 27 STH, Regeringsgatan 12,
DS STOCKHOLM. ☎08/23 89 00

SWITZERLAND – SUISSE
Librairie Payot, 6 rue Grenus, 1211 GENÈVE 11. ☎022-31.89.50

TAIWAN – FORMOSE
National Book Company,
84-5 Sing Sung Rd., Sec. 3, TAIPEI 107. ☎321.0698

TURKEY – TURQUIE
Librairie Hachette,
469 Istiklal Caddesi, Beyoglu, ISTANBUL. ☎44.94.70
et 14 E Ziya Gökalp Caddesi, ANKARA. ☎12.10.80

UNITED KINGDOM – ROYAUME-UNI
H.M. Stationery Office, P.O.B. 569,
LONDON SE1 9 NH. ☎01-928-6977, Ext.410
or
49 High Holborn, LONDON WC1V 6 HB (personal callers)
Branches at: EDINBURGH, BIRMINGHAM, BRISTOL,
MANCHESTER, CARDIFF, BELFAST.

UNITED STATES OF AMERICA
OECD Publications Center, Suite 1207, 1750 Pennsylvania Ave.,
N.W. WASHINGTON, D.C.20006. ☎(202)298-8755

VENEZUELA
Libreria del Este, Avda. F. Miranda 52, Edificio Galipán,
CARACAS 106. ☎32 23 01/33 26 04/33 24 73

YUGOSLAVIA – YOUGOSLAVIE
Jugoslovenska Knjiga, Terazije 27, P.O.B. 36, BEOGRAD.
☎621-992

Les commandes provenant de pays où l'OCDE n'a pas encore désigné de dépositaire peuvent être adressées à :
OCDE, Bureau des Publications, 2 rue André-Pascal, 75775 PARIS CEDEX 16.
Orders and inquiries from countries where sales agents have not yet been appointed may be sent to:
OECD, Publications Office, 2 rue André-Pascal, 75775 PARIS CEDEX 16.

OECD PUBLICATIONS
2, rue André-Pascal, 75775 Paris Cedex 16

No. 40.029 1977

PRINTED IN FRANCE